Worship in the Marketplace, Worship Beyond the Walls

(Turning Work into Worship)

Gerard Assey

Worship in the Marketplace,
Worship Beyond the Walls:
(Turning Work into Worship)

By
Gerard Assey

Published by:
Gerard Assey
19/18, Palli Arasan Street
Anna Nagar East
Chennai - 600 102

ISBN: 978-81-993017-3-3

Table of Contents

Preface

Worship has long been portrayed as something that happens on Sundays, within the walls of a church, accompanied by music, candles, and liturgy. While there is beauty in formal worship, the Bible reveals a far richer truth: worship is not a place, a time, or even an activity—it is a lifestyle. It is the act of aligning our hearts, actions, and ambitions with God's presence, no matter where we are or what we are doing.

The inspiration for this book came from observing the quiet, often unnoticed ways God's people worship in their everyday lives. I have seen it in the nurse who prays over every patient before starting her shift, the student who chooses integrity over shortcuts in exams, the business owner who treats his employees with honor and fairness even when it costs profit. These acts, ordinary to human eyes, are extraordinary in the sight of God. They demonstrate that every workplace, classroom, hospital, and street can become an altar for His glory.

In the pages that follow, you will be invited to reimagine worship beyond the church walls. Each chapter is carefully crafted to connect Scripture with practical life, weaving together stories from the Old and New Testaments with real-life examples of modern believers, all fictitious but grounded in reality. From Joseph and Daniel, who carried God's presence into pagan systems, to a young professional turning a corporate office into a place of daily devotion, the thread is clear: worship thrives wherever God's presence is acknowledged and honored.

This book is not meant to be read passively. It is meant to be experienced, applied, and lived out. You will find reflection exercises, practical tools, and action steps at the end of chapters to help you take the truths of Scripture and apply them in your own sphere of influence. Whether you are a teacher, student, business professional, government servant, or homemaker, the call remains the same: to live a life that sings, even when no one is listening, and to bring heaven into your everyday spaces.

My prayer is that by the end of this book, you will see your life, your work, and your relationships through a different lens—a lens that recognizes that every place can be holy, every task can be an offering, and every act of obedience can be worship.
May your life become a song of praise that resonates beyond the walls of the sanctuary, filling your workplace, your community, and ultimately, the world.

— **Gerard Assey**

Introduction: Worship Without Walls

There was a time when worship was thought to be confined within stone walls—echoing through stained glass windows, reverberating with music, and punctuated by "Amens." Many still carry that picture in their minds: worship as what happens on Sunday mornings, with lifted hands, closed eyes, and a band playing softly in the background. But the truth is, God never designed worship to be an event. Worship was always meant to be a way of life.

Jesus broke this misconception when He spoke to a Samaritan woman beside a well in John 4:23–24. He said, *"Yet a time is coming and has now come when the true worshippers will worship the Father in spirit and in truth, for they are the kind of worshippers the Father seeks. God is spirit, and His worshippers must worship in the Spirit and in truth."*

Here was a woman who thought worship was about a location — the mountain for the Samaritans, or Jerusalem for the Jews. Jesus shattered that notion by revealing that true worship transcends geography, rituals, and routines. Worship is not about where you stand, but about how you live.

Paul would later reinforce this truth in Romans 12:1, when he wrote: *"Therefore, I urge you, brothers and sisters, in view of God's mercy, to offer your bodies as a living sacrifice, holy and acceptable to God— this is your true and proper worship."* Notice, Paul doesn't mention a song, a melody, or a gathering. He speaks of a life offered — a body, a mind, a heart fully yielded to God in every moment.

Worship, therefore, is not merely an act we perform; it is an attitude we live by. It is not limited to songs sung but includes decisions made, attitudes displayed, and values upheld when no one else is watching.

Worship as an Act vs. Worship as a Lifestyle
We often think of worship as a Sunday activity: singing, clapping, raising hands, maybe even shedding a tear or two during a heartfelt chorus. That is worship as an act, and it is important. But there is a higher dimension — worship as a lifestyle. Worship as an act is momentary; worship as a lifestyle is continuous. The former is expressed through a song; the latter is expressed through obedience, excellence, and service.

Noah's worship began long before he built an altar after the flood — it started when he obeyed God's strange command to build a massive ark in the middle of dry land. Abraham's worship did not begin when he named the mountain "The Lord Will Provide." It began when he got up early the next morning to climb Mount Moriah, knife in hand, fully surrendered to God's will. In both cases, worship wasn't limited to a song or ceremony. It was obedience expressed through action.

Similarly, in the New Testament, Mary of Bethany's act of pouring expensive perfume on Jesus' feet was more than an emotional outburst; it was a lifestyle statement. She gave her best, not for recognition but for love. Her worship filled the room, not just with fragrance but with reverence. Her act was public, but her motive was deeply personal. That is what God desires — worship that flows from a surrendered heart, not a rehearsed ritual.

The Marketplace: God's New Mission Field

If worship is a lifestyle, then the world is the stage. The marketplace — where we spend most of our waking hours — is where this worship must find its expression. God never intended the world to be divided into "sacred" and "secular." That distinction was man-made. When Jesus called His disciples, He didn't recruit them from temples but from fishing boats, tax booths, and city streets. He turned ordinary workplaces into places of divine encounter.

When Joseph served in Potiphar's house and later in Pharaoh's palace, he wasn't preaching sermons or leading worship songs. Yet his integrity, diligence, and excellence became acts of worship that honoured God and impacted an entire nation. The same Spirit that filled the temple later filled the workplace through Joseph's faithfulness. Daniel too worshipped God not through public praise, but through private devotion and public excellence. Even when Babylon tried to rename him, retrain him, and reshape him, Daniel remained unmoved in his inner allegiance. His worship was unshaken by the environment around him.

Today's believers are called to that same kind of worship — not confined to pews and pulpits but released into boardrooms, classrooms, and construction sites. The classroom can become a sanctuary, the office a tabernacle, and the shop floor a holy ground when God is glorified there.

Rohan's Story – When Work Becomes Worship

Rohan was a young marketing executive working in a competitive firm in Mumbai. His world revolved around targets, deadlines, and clients who demanded more than they paid for. Sundays were his "God time," and the rest of the week belonged to business. But deep within, he felt a growing emptiness.

One day, after a particularly harsh confrontation with a client, Rohan sat at his desk, exhausted. His anger simmered from being blamed unfairly. Just then, his eyes fell on a sticky note he had written months ago from a Sunday sermon: *"Whatever you do, work at it with all your heart, as working for the Lord, not for men."* (Colossians 3:23)

That verse hit differently that day. What if his work could actually be an act of worship? What if the way he treated clients — even unreasonable ones — was part of his offering to God? That thought stirred something new.

The next day, Rohan consciously decided to change how he worked. He began to pray before starting his day, asking God for grace to serve people well. Instead of reacting in frustration, he started responding in patience. His emails became kinder, his presentations more thoughtful, his integrity stronger. Over time, his colleagues noticed something different — not just his work ethic, but his peace.

One evening, his boss asked, *"Rohan, what changed? You used to be so tense all the time."* Rohan smiled. *"I realized I'm not just working for a company anymore. I'm working for God."*

That's when work became worship.

Worship moved from Sunday morning songs to Monday morning spreadsheets. The sacred flowed into the secular. Rohan hadn't changed jobs; he had changed altars. And suddenly, every client meeting, every presentation, every act of patience became incense rising before the Lord.

Every Place Becomes Sacred When God is Glorified There

Worship is not about where you are but Whom you carry. When you walk into your office, school, or shop, you bring the presence of God with you. The same Spirit that hovered over the waters in Genesis now lives in you. When you walk into a meeting with integrity, when you serve a customer with kindness, when you forgive a colleague who wrongs you — you are worshipping God in truth.

Jacob once fell asleep in a desolate place, using a stone as his pillow. When he woke up, he declared, *"Surely the Lord is in this place, and I was not aware of it!"* (Genesis 28:16). The place had not changed — his perception had. What was ordinary became sacred because he recognized God's presence there.

In the same way, your office, your classroom, your kitchen, your cab, or your marketplace can become sacred spaces when you choose to glorify God there. Worship, then, is not what happens when the music starts; it's what continues when the music stops.

As you turn these pages, may your understanding of worship expand. May your heart catch the revelation that your work, your words, and your world are altars of worship. For when your life becomes the song, God becomes the audience.

Chapter 1:
From Sanctuary to Street – Redefining Worship

For many believers, the word "worship" immediately paints a familiar picture — a congregation standing with raised hands, music swelling, voices lifted, and hearts moved. It's beautiful and sacred. Yet, for all its beauty, this picture captures only a fraction of what worship truly is. Worship was never meant to be confined within the four walls of a sanctuary; it was meant to spill out into the streets, into homes, offices, classrooms, and communities.

Paul's words in Colossians 3 reshape our understanding of this truth: *"Whatever you do, in word or deed, do it all in the name of the Lord Jesus, giving thanks to God the Father through Him... Whatever you do, work at it with all your heart, as working for the Lord, not for human masters, since you know that you will receive an inheritance from the Lord as a reward. It is the Lord Christ you are serving."* (Colossians 3:17, 23–24)

Paul does not say, *"Whatever you sing."* He says, *"Whatever you do."* That means everything — from the way we greet our colleagues to the way we conduct business, raise children, study, and treat others — can become an act of worship when done with a heart that seeks to honour God.

When Worship Moves Beyond the Building

For centuries, Israel's worship was centered around a physical place — the Tabernacle, then later the

Temple in Jerusalem. These were magnificent spaces where sacrifices were offered, incense burned, and songs were sung to the Lord. The sanctuary symbolized God's dwelling among His people. But over time, something tragic happened. Worship became more about the place than the Person. People began equating proximity to the temple with proximity to God.

In Isaiah 58, God confronted this mindset. The people were fasting, praying, and bowing low, but God was displeased. He said, *"Is this the kind of fast I have chosen… only for a man to bow his head like a reed? Is not this the kind of fasting I have chosen: to loose the chains of injustice, to set the oppressed free and break every yoke?"* (Isaiah 58:5–6)

Through the prophet Isaiah, God was declaring that true worship is not merely what happens in the sanctuary; it's what happens in society. It's the justice we pursue, the compassion we show, and the integrity we uphold when no one is watching. Worship that stays within church walls is incomplete. It must extend to how we treat people — our employees, customers, neighbours, even strangers.

God was saying, *"Don't just sing to Me; live for Me. Don't just raise your hands; extend them to the poor, the broken, and the weary."* Worship must move from the sanctuary to the street — from songs to service.

David: A Worshipper Beyond the Harp

David is often remembered as the man who played the harp, wrote psalms, and danced before the Lord. And while that is true, his worship extended far beyond melodies and music. It was expressed through his leadership, courage, and heart after God.

When David tended his father's sheep in the hills of Bethlehem, he was already a worshipper. Alone under the stars, his harp echoed songs of trust and dependence on God. But that same worship showed up in his courage when he faced Goliath, declaring, *"You come to me with sword and spear, but I come to you in the name of the Lord of hosts."* (1 Samuel 17:45)

Later, as a king, David's worship was seen not just in the songs he wrote, but in the justice he pursued and the mercy he extended. When he showed kindness to Mephibosheth, the crippled son of Jonathan, it was an act of worship rooted in loyalty and compassion. Even when he failed — as he did grievously — his repentance in Psalm 51 revealed a heart that valued God's presence more than position or power.

David teaches us that worship is not a genre of music; it is a posture of life. It can be expressed in quiet devotion or in bold leadership, in repentance or in victory, in shepherding sheep or ruling a nation. His life reveals that worship is not confined to sacred spaces; it is lived out in every responsibility God places in our hands.

The Early Church: Worship Without a Building

In the New Testament, worship took a new shape. When the early believers received the Holy Spirit, their gatherings looked very different from what we often imagine today. Acts 2:46–47 describes it beautifully: *"Every day they continued to meet together in the temple courts. They broke bread in their homes and ate together with glad and sincere hearts, praising God and enjoying the favour of all the people."*

Their worship was alive and mobile — it moved from the temple courts into homes, markets, and streets. The believers didn't wait for Sunday; they worshipped through their daily lives. They shared food, helped the poor, and encouraged one another in faith. Their worship became their witness.

There were no elaborate stages, lighting, or choirs — yet the presence of God was tangible. Every meal became a communion table, every home a sanctuary. Worship was not about a "service" they attended, but a *life* they lived. And as they lived that way, Scripture says, *"The Lord added to their number daily those who were being saved."* Their authentic, lived-out worship drew people to Jesus more than any program ever could.

The early believers redefined worship for all generations to come: it's not limited to where you gather, but to Whom you belong.

Meera's Story – When Teaching Became an Altar

Meera had been a schoolteacher for over fifteen years in a small town. She loved her students but often felt frustrated by the system — the bureaucracy, the lack of resources, and at times, the indifference of parents. Over the years, she had begun to separate her "spiritual life" from her "work life." Sundays were for church; Mondays were for survival.

One evening, while preparing her lesson plans, she came across Colossians 3:23–24 during her devotional time: *"Whatever you do, work at it with all your heart, as working for the Lord, not for human masters."* She paused. Could her teaching really be her act of worship? Could her classroom become her altar?

The next morning, she decided to try something different. Before her students arrived, she whispered a simple prayer: *"Lord, today, I teach for You."* That day, her perspective changed. She taught with renewed joy and patience. When a slow learner stumbled, she encouraged instead of scolded. When her colleagues complained about the workload, she smiled and quietly helped them.

Weeks passed, and something began to shift. Her students responded with more enthusiasm; her classroom felt lighter. Parents began noticing changes in their children. One parent told her, *"Ma'am, my son says you make him feel seen."* Meera smiled, knowing that what had changed wasn't her students — it was her heart.

Meera's classroom had become her sanctuary. Her whiteboard was her pulpit; her students were her congregation. Every equation solved, every paper graded, every word of encouragement offered became a note in her song of worship to God.

She had moved worship from Sunday to Monday — from sanctuary to street — and discovered that the same Spirit she encountered in church was with her at her desk.

True Worship: When Every Day Becomes Holy

The heart of worship is not measured by how passionately we sing on Sunday but by how faithfully we live on Monday. Worship begins when the music fades and the real world begins — when you choose patience over anger, forgiveness over revenge, diligence over laziness, and truth over convenience.

Every time you honour God in your work, care for someone in need, act with integrity when no one sees, or love the unlovable — you are worshipping

Him. Worship is the offering of your daily life to a God who sees your heart.

The street, the shop, the classroom, the kitchen, the office — all can become extensions of the sanctuary. When we carry God's presence into the everyday, we bridge the sacred and the secular. The true measure of worship is not how loud we sing but how deeply we love, how honestly we live, and how wholeheartedly we serve.

So remember this: ***worship doesn't start on Sunday—it starts on Monday.***

And perhaps, when believers begin to live this truth, the world will begin to see church not as a building we go to, but as a people who carry the presence of God wherever they go.

Chapter 2: The Marketplace Mandate – God's Presence in Public Spaces

For far too long, many believers have lived with an invisible wall dividing their faith from their work. On one side lies what they call "spiritual life"—church, prayer, worship, and ministry. On the other side sits "secular life"—work, business, study, politics, and public affairs. But the truth is, in God's eyes, there is no such divide. All of life is sacred when it is surrendered to Him.

God never intended His people to withdraw from the world but to transform it from within. The marketplace—the place where people buy, sell, govern, build, learn, and create—was always meant to be a stage where His glory would be revealed. From the beginning of time, God's presence was not limited to temples or altars. In Genesis, we see Him walking with Adam in the garden—a workplace, not a worship hall.

The true test of worship, therefore, is not how powerfully we encounter God in the sanctuary, but how consistently we carry Him into the spaces where His name is rarely mentioned.

God in the Workplace: The Story of Joseph

Few lives illustrate the presence of God in public spaces more powerfully than Joseph's. The young dreamer, sold into slavery by his own brothers, found himself in Egypt—a land known for idolatry and corruption. Yet, despite being in an ungodly environment, Scripture says something remarkable about him:

"The Lord was with Joseph, and he prospered... When his master saw that the Lord was with him and that the Lord gave him success in everything he did, Joseph found favor in his eyes and became his attendant." (Genesis 39:2–3)

Joseph's life teaches us that God's presence is not restricted by location. You can be in the palace or in prison, in the marketplace or in ministry—if God is with you, His favor will follow you. Joseph did not wait to be in a temple to worship; his worship was seen in how he worked, how he led, and how he forgave.

Even when falsely accused and thrown into prison, Joseph continued to serve faithfully. His integrity was his altar, his excellence his incense. Eventually, his faithfulness elevated him from the dungeon to the throne room. He became Pharaoh's chief administrator, managing the economy of an entire nation and saving millions from famine—including his own family.

Joseph's story reminds us that God can use our workplaces as pulpits and our professions as platforms for His purpose. When the world sees integrity, wisdom, and compassion in us, they experience a glimpse of His presence.

Your office, your classroom, your business—these are not distractions from your calling; they are the very places where your calling unfolds.

Daniel in Babylon: Excellence as Evidence

Centuries later, another young man found himself in a similar position. Daniel, taken captive to Babylon, was forced to serve a pagan king in a foreign land.

Yet rather than resist his assignment, he decided to represent God within it.

"Now Daniel so distinguished himself among the administrators and the satraps by his exceptional qualities that the king planned to set him over the whole kingdom." (Daniel 6:3)

Daniel's distinction wasn't because of his title or connections—it was because of the Spirit of God upon him. He didn't separate his faith from his function. His prayers shaped his performance. His integrity became his influence.

When laws were passed to outlaw prayer, Daniel didn't compromise. He didn't hide his devotion, nor did he flaunt it; he simply continued his daily rhythm of worship—three times a day, as usual. His faithfulness led him to the lion's den, but even there, God's presence prevailed.

Daniel's story tells us that true worshippers influence culture without being influenced by it. Babylon couldn't corrupt him because his allegiance was anchored in heaven. He was a worshipper disguised as a statesman, a man who understood that his role in government was as sacred as the priest's role in the temple.

The marketplace today needs modern Daniels—men and women who carry excellence, integrity, and the fear of God into boardrooms, classrooms, and corridors of power.

Esther in Persia: Courage for a Cause

Esther's life unfolds in yet another secular setting—the Persian palace. She was a young Jewish woman who became queen in a foreign empire, completely surrounded by luxury, politics, and paganism. But when the lives of her people were threatened by

Haman's wicked decree, Esther was faced with a defining choice: stay silent for her own comfort or speak up for God's purpose.

Her cousin Mordecai's words still echo across generations: *"Who knows but that you have come to your royal position for such a time as this?"* (Esther 4:14)

With courage anchored in faith, Esther risked her life to approach the king uninvited—a bold move that could have cost her everything. Yet that act of obedience changed history. She didn't deliver a sermon or perform a miracle. She simply acted in faith, using her position, influence, and wisdom to protect God's people.

Esther teaches us that God places His worshippers in unexpected spaces for divine purposes. You may be a teacher, a manager, a government officer, or an entrepreneur—your position is not accidental. You are there "for such a time as this." Worship happens when you recognize that your job is your ministry and your influence is your assignment.

Jesus in the Streets: Worship That Walks

Even in the New Testament, we see Jesus Himself taking worship into the streets. He taught in synagogues, yes, but He also preached from fishing boats, healed in marketplaces, ate with tax collectors, and turned wellsides into sanctuaries. He met people in their daily routines—at work, in crowds, on roadsides.

For Jesus, every space was sacred because every soul mattered. His ministry was not confined to a pulpit; it pulsed through the ordinary moments of life. When He told Peter to cast his net after a night of failure, He transformed a fisherman's workplace into a place of revelation. When He called Matthew from his tax booth, He turned a desk of corruption into a table of redemption.

That is the heart of the marketplace mandate: to make God visible where He is least expected.

Modern Story: When Ethics Became Worship

Rakesh was the CEO of a growing logistics company in Bangalore. His business was thriving, but as competition increased, so did the pressure to cut corners. A major government contract was within reach—but there was a catch. A senior official subtly hinted that the deal would only go through if a "gift" changed hands.

Rakesh's management team urged him to comply. *"It's just how business works here,"* they said. *"If we don't do it, our rivals will."* But Rakesh couldn't silence the conviction in his heart. He spent the night in prayer, wrestling between profit and principle.

As he read Daniel 6 that morning, one verse stood out: *"They could find no corruption in him, because he was trustworthy and neither corrupt nor negligent."* (Daniel 6:4) He realized that the greatest offering he could give God that day was integrity.

Rakesh declined the bribe. The deal was lost, and so were several short-term opportunities. But over time, his company developed a reputation for honesty and reliability. Years later, when the same department needed a trustworthy partner for a high-value project, Rakesh's company was their first choice.

When asked by a journalist how he had built such credibility, he smiled and said, *"By putting worship before wealth. Every decision in my company is an offering to God."*

Rakesh understood that his office was his mission field, his boardroom his altar, and his business decisions his sacrifices of praise.

Turning Daily Assignments into Divine Assignments

When we begin to see our work as worship, everything changes. The mundane becomes meaningful, and the routine becomes sacred. The call of God is not always to leave your job for ministry; often, it is to bring ministry into your job.

Your assignment as a believer is not limited to singing hymns on Sunday; it's to carry His presence into your school on Monday, your shop on Tuesday, your meetings on Wednesday, and your community every day after.

Colossians 3:17 reminds us, *"Whatever you do, in word or deed, do it all in the name of the Lord Jesus."* That means every email you write, every call you answer, every plan you execute can become an offering of worship when done with the right heart.

Imagine what could happen if every believer began to see their workplace as their worship space—where teachers prayed over their students, entrepreneurs built businesses on kingdom values, and employees worked with excellence as though Jesus Himself were their boss. The world would see the light of Christ not through sermons, but through lives that shine with His presence.

The Mandate Restored

God is raising a new generation of worshippers who understand that the church is not a building we go to, but a people we are. He is reclaiming the marketplace as His mission field and calling believers to bring His presence into public spaces—schools, hospitals, media, politics, and business.

You are not merely a worker; you are an ambassador. You are not simply earning a living; you are revealing the Kingdom. When you step into your workplace, you carry the same Spirit that hovered over the waters in Genesis, the same wisdom that guided Joseph, the same excellence that distinguished Daniel, and the same courage that empowered Esther.

So, as you walk into your day tomorrow, remember: you are not just clocking in—you are being sent.

Every assignment can become a divine assignment when done for the glory of God.

When God's people understand this, the walls between church and marketplace will finally crumble, and the earth will begin to echo with worship—not just from sanctuaries, but from schools, offices, homes, and every place where His children carry His name.

Chapter 3: Work as Worship – Excellence as an Offering

When most people hear the word *worship*, they imagine singing, lifting hands, or kneeling in prayer. But what if worship was never meant to be confined to a song, a posture, or a Sunday service? What if worship was meant to be the way you sweep your floor, teach your students, code your program, write your report, or manage your business?

True worship begins when your work becomes your offering.

God never separates sacred from secular. In His eyes, the way a preacher prepares a sermon and the way a carpenter shapes a table can both glorify Him—if done with the same devotion. The question is not *what* you do, but *for whom* you do it.

Paul captured this truth beautifully when he wrote,

"Whatever you do, work at it with all your heart, as working for the Lord, not for human masters." (Colossians 3:23)

When you begin to see your work as worship, everything changes. Excellence becomes an act of reverence. Diligence becomes devotion. Integrity becomes incense before God.

The Call to Excellence

Proverbs 22:29 says, *"Do you see a man skilled in his work? He will stand before kings; he will not stand before obscure men."*

Skill, diligence, and excellence are not worldly qualities—they are spiritual virtues. God takes pleasure in excellence because it reflects His own nature. From the intricate design of a snowflake to the vast order of the galaxies, everything He made displays precision and beauty. Excellence is not perfection—it is stewardship. It is doing the best you can with what God has entrusted to you, in the way that honors Him most.

To work with excellence is to say, *"Lord, this is for You."*

Bezalel: The Craftsman Filled with the Spirit

Our first biblical example of someone *filled with the Spirit* is not a prophet or priest—it's a craftsman.

In Exodus 31:1–5, God says to Moses: *"See, I have chosen Bezalel… and I have filled him with the Spirit of God, with wisdom, understanding, knowledge and all kinds of skills—to make artistic designs for work in gold, silver and bronze."*

Bezalel's assignment was not to preach or to lead worship—it was to build. Yet God saw his craftsmanship as holy work. The Spirit that anointed prophets to speak also anointed Bezalel to design. His chisels and hammers became instruments of worship.

Imagine the sound of Bezalel's hammer echoing through the camp of Israel—not as noise, but as praise. Every carving, every engraving, every measured cut was a testimony that God values excellence.

Bezalel's story reminds us that worship is not limited to words; it's revealed in workmanship. When we do our work with integrity and skill, we mirror the Creator Himself—the first and greatest worker. Genesis 2 tells us that God *"finished His work"* and then rested, declaring it "*very good.*" God was satisfied not merely

because He had completed something, but because it reflected His character.
When you give your best effort, you are reflecting the nature of a God who does all things well.

Paul the Tentmaker: Ministry Through Marketplace
The Apostle Paul is best known for his letters and missionary journeys, but tucked quietly in Acts 18:3 is a powerful truth:
"Because he was of the same trade, he stayed with them and worked, for they were tentmakers by trade."
Even while preaching the gospel across nations, Paul earned his living by making tents. He didn't see manual labor as beneath him. His tent-making was not a distraction from ministry—it *was* ministry. Through it, he modeled humility, discipline, and the integration of faith and work.
Paul's life teaches us that sacred purpose can flow through ordinary work. Whether stitching fabric or preaching truth, his motive was the same—to glorify Christ.
He once told the Thessalonians, *"We worked night and day, laboring and toiling so that we would not be a burden to any of you."* (2 Thessalonians 3:8)
In other words, his work ethic was part of his witness. The same hands that wrote epistles also shaped canvas. That is what worship looks like in motion—spirit and sweat working together for God's glory.

Anita's Story: When Coding Became Worship
Anita was a software developer in a fast-paced tech company in Mumbai. Her life was a blur of deadlines, coffee, and computer screens. Though she loved

God deeply, she often felt her job had little spiritual value. "What does writing code have to do with worship?" she would ask herself.

Over time, the pressure to meet targets began to change her habits. She started cutting corners—copying snippets from others' work, skipping quality checks, and delivering projects just "good enough." Her supervisors were satisfied, but deep down, Anita knew she was compromising.

One evening, after a particularly hectic day, she opened her Bible and came across Matthew 25:21: *"Well done, good and faithful servant."*

The words struck her differently that night. She imagined Jesus looking at her—not as a church volunteer or worship singer—but as a coder. Could she really say she was giving Him her best?

The next morning, Anita prayed a simple prayer at her desk: *"Lord, today I will code as unto You."*

From that day on, everything changed. She began reviewing her work more carefully, documenting thoroughly, and designing with thoughtfulness. She stopped taking shortcuts. She treated every line of code as if it were her offering to God.

When colleagues asked why she cared so much about small details, she smiled and said, "Because this is my worship."

Her excellence began to speak louder than her words. Over time, her integrity and skill earned her respect, promotions, and—more importantly—opportunities to share her faith. A simple shift in perspective had turned her workplace into a place of worship.

Integrity: The Fragrance of True Worship

In a world where shortcuts are celebrated, integrity is a rare perfume. Yet, it is the aroma God cherishes most. The excellence that pleases Him is not just in performance, but in purity.

It's possible to work efficiently yet dishonestly; to deliver results but lack righteousness. But God measures not just *what* we do, but *how* we do it. Proverbs 10:9 says, *"Whoever walks in integrity walks securely."*

When you sign an honest report, return what doesn't belong to you, refuse to exaggerate numbers, or own up to a mistake—you are worshipping God. Your integrity becomes your incense.

The world may not understand it, but heaven does. Every honest act is a silent song of praise.

Excellence as Worship, Not Performance

It's important to understand that excellence is not about impressing people or striving for perfection. It's about honoring God. The difference lies in the motive.

Performance seeks applause. Worship seeks approval—from the only One whose opinion matters.

Excellence in God's eyes means doing your best with the resources, time, and strength you have, and leaving the results in His hands. When we work this way, we free ourselves from anxiety and comparison. We no longer need validation from bosses or peers; our reward comes from the Lord Himself.

That's why Jesus told the faithful servant in His parable, *"Well done, good and faithful servant."* (Matthew 25:21) He didn't say, "Well known" or "Well noticed." Faithfulness—not fame—is what God celebrates.

A Work Desk as an Altar

If your heart is God's temple, your desk can be His altar.

Try this simple act of dedication. Tomorrow morning, before you begin work, pause for a moment. Lay your hand on your computer, your books, your tools, or whatever represents your craft. Whisper this prayer:

"Lord, I dedicate this space to You. May every thought, task, and word from this desk honor Your name. Let my work today be an offering, my diligence a song, my integrity a sacrifice of praise.

This is not just a workstation—it's an altar of worship."

That quiet consecration will shift your mindset. Suddenly, the mundane becomes holy. Your spreadsheets become psalms. Your reports become testimonies.

Because in the Kingdom, every desk can become a sanctuary.

The Takeaway

When we work with excellence, diligence, and integrity, we declare something powerful about our God—that He is worthy of our best.

Bezalel built the Tabernacle with divine precision. Paul made tents with holy purpose. Anita coded with reverence. You, too, can transform your daily labor into a divine liturgy.

The true measure of a worshipper is not only how they lift their hands in church, but how they use those same hands from Monday to Saturday.

- ✓ *Your excellence is your offering.*
- ✓ *Your diligence is your devotion.*

- ✓ *Your integrity is your incense.*

And when you work as unto the Lord, heaven looks down and whispers, *“Well done.”*

Chapter 4: Worship through Integrity – When No One is Watching

If worship is the fragrance that rises to heaven, then integrity is the incense that keeps it pure. Without integrity, our songs lose their sweetness, and our offerings lose their meaning. Integrity is the hidden worship — the kind that happens when no one applauds, no one sees, and no one but God knows.

In a world filled with shortcuts, half-truths, and shifting morals, living uprightly can seem old-fashioned or even naïve. But in God's Kingdom, integrity is still the standard. It's not optional — it's essential. Psalm 15 paints a clear picture of the kind of person who can dwell in God's presence:

"Lord, who may dwell in your sacred tent? Who may live on your holy mountain?
The one whose walk is blameless,
who does what is righteous,
who speaks the truth from his heart…
Whoever does these things will never be shaken." (Psalm 15:1–2, 5)

David understood something profound — God's presence is not sustained by performance, but by purity. Worship that lacks integrity is empty noise. But worship backed by character becomes a sweet aroma that moves the heart of God.

Integrity: The Hidden Foundation of True Worship

Integrity simply means *wholeness* — to be undivided, the same inside and out. The Hebrew word "tamim," often translated as "blameless," carries the sense of being complete, sound, or perfect in one's heart before God.

It's possible to sing beautifully on Sunday and still cheat subtly on Monday. It's possible to pray fervently in public and yet cut corners in private. But that's not the kind of worship God desires. Proverbs 11:1 reminds us:

"Dishonest scales are detestable to the Lord, but accurate weights find favor with Him."

This verse isn't just about business transactions; it's about moral balance. God detests duplicity — when what we show outside doesn't match what's inside. Worship without integrity is like perfume poured into a cracked vessel — it cannot hold its fragrance.

Integrity is not tested in the crowd, but in solitude. The question is not how we behave when people watch, but how we live when no one does.

Joseph: Integrity in a Hidden Room

Few stories illustrate integrity better than that of Joseph in Genesis 39. A young man, far from home, stripped of his comfort and reputation, serving as a slave in Potiphar's house. Despite his circumstances, Joseph's integrity remained intact. Scripture says:

"The Lord was with Joseph, and he prospered... When his master saw that the Lord was with him... Joseph found favor in his eyes." (Genesis 39:2–4)

Joseph's integrity brought him favor — but it was also what got him into trouble. When Potiphar's wife tried to seduce him, Joseph faced the ultimate test: the kind that comes when there's no one to impress and no one to defend you.

He could have rationalized it: "No one will know. I deserve this. I've been treated unfairly anyway." But Joseph's answer revealed his worshipful heart:
"How then can I do this great wickedness and sin against God?" (Genesis 39:9)
Notice what he said — *"against God."* Joseph's understanding of worship went far beyond rituals. His integrity wasn't loyalty to Potiphar or to moral rules — it was devotion to God Himself. For Joseph, sin was not just a violation of law; it was a betrayal of relationship.
He fled temptation, not because he feared exposure, but because he loved God too much to grieve Him. That's worship. True integrity flows from intimacy with God — the awareness that His presence is always near.
Even when Joseph was falsely accused and imprisoned, his integrity remained unbroken. And in time, that same integrity elevated him to govern Egypt. His worship in private prepared him for his witness in public.

Integrity in the New Testament: The Hidden Life of Jesus

Even Jesus modeled integrity long before He began His public ministry. For thirty years, He lived quietly in Nazareth as a carpenter — working with His hands, obeying His parents, and living blamelessly before God and man. Scripture doesn't record any miracles during that period, yet it tells us He *"grew in wisdom and stature, and in favor with God and men."* (Luke 2:52)
Those silent years were years of integrity. Jesus didn't need applause to be faithful. His hidden

obedience was as much worship as His public preaching.

When tempted by Satan in the wilderness (Matthew 4), Jesus again demonstrated integrity. The devil offered Him shortcuts — to satisfy hunger, to gain fame, to seize power without the cross. But Jesus chose the narrow path of obedience. He refused to compromise even when no one else was watching.

Integrity is forged in the wilderness — in the moments of testing, when the easy option conflicts with the right one.

Rajesh's Story: Integrity in the Office

Rajesh was a senior finance manager in a mid-sized manufacturing company. Over the years, he had built a reputation for being thorough, disciplined, and dependable. His faith was quiet but steady — he believed in doing what was right, even when it wasn't popular.

One financial quarter, the company faced a major audit. The CEO, anxious to show better numbers, called Rajesh into his office. *"Just adjust a few figures,"* he said casually. "*It's not really cheating — just creative accounting. We'll fix it next quarter."*

Rajesh felt his stomach twist. He knew this was wrong. Yet he also knew refusing could cost him his job — and the promotion he'd been waiting years for. He took a deep breath and replied gently, "Sir, I'm afraid I can't do that. It wouldn't be honest before God or before the board."

The room fell silent. The CEO frowned. *"You're being too rigid, Rajesh. Everyone does it."*

But Rajesh stood his ground. He left the office feeling both anxious and at peace. A week later, the promotion went to someone else. Rumors began circulating that Rajesh was "too spiritual" and "not practical enough."

Months passed, and the audit uncovered financial discrepancies from another department. The company's leadership was shaken. It was Rajesh's accurate and transparent books that helped restore credibility. Eventually, the CEO called him back in — this time to apologize.

"Rajesh," he said quietly, *"you did the right thing. I see that now. We need more people like you."*

Rajesh smiled, knowing the reward that mattered most had already been given — the quiet approval of his Master.

That evening, as he drove home, he whispered a simple prayer: *"Lord, I did this for You."* His integrity had become his worship.

Integrity: The Incense that Rises Before God

Integrity is unseen worship — the kind that burns quietly but fills heaven with fragrance. Every time you refuse to lie, return what isn't yours, keep your promise, or admit your fault, a fresh whiff of holy incense rises before God.

God doesn't measure integrity by outcomes but by obedience. Joseph's integrity led him to prison before it led him to promotion. Rajesh's integrity cost him advancement before it earned him respect. But in every case, heaven was watching — and favor followed.

Psalm 15 promises that those who walk uprightly "shall never be moved." Integrity anchors your life in stability because it aligns you with God's unchanging nature. People may misunderstand, systems may fail you, but when your heart is true, your foundation is firm.

An "Integrity Inventory" for Daily Life

Worship through integrity is not a one-time act; it's a daily decision. It's choosing truth in small things so that when big tests come, your character stands firm. Here's a simple reflection exercise — a personal Integrity Inventory you can quietly ask yourself each day:

- ✓ *Am I the same person in private as I am in public? (Integrity means being consistent when no one is watching.)*
- ✓ *Have I been fully truthful today — in words, reports, promises, and commitments?*
- ✓ *Have I handled money, time, and responsibilities as if they belonged to God — because they do?*
- ✓ *Have I honored others in my speech, even when they are not present?*
- ✓ *Have I made peace where there was tension, and forgiveness where there was hurt?*
- ✓ *Would I be comfortable if Jesus reviewed every decision I made today?*
- ✓ *Have I kept my heart free from bitterness, greed, or hidden compromise?*

You don't have to be perfect — but you must be honest. Integrity isn't about never falling; it's about never faking. When you stumble, confess quickly and rise again. The heart that seeks truth will always find grace.

When Heaven Smiles

Integrity may not always bring applause, but it always brings approval — from the only One whose opinion truly matters.

When you choose honesty in the face of pressure, purity in the midst of temptation, and righteousness over recognition — heaven smiles.
Because in that moment, you're doing what angels do — offering worship before the throne, not with songs or instruments, but with a life that pleases the heart of God.

So live with this conviction: Integrity is worship when no one is watching. And remember — what is done in secret will one day be celebrated in glory.

Chapter 5: The Worshipper's Attitude – Gratitude, Humility, and Servanthood

Worship is not just the song we sing, the hands we lift, or the words we speak—it's the posture of our heart in every moment of life. When Jesus described the kind of worship the Father seeks, He wasn't merely speaking of style or sound. He was speaking of spirit—an inner disposition marked by gratitude, humility, and servanthood. True worship is reflected not in how loudly we sing on Sunday, but in how lovingly we serve on Monday.

The Heart Posture of a Worshipper

The Apostle Paul captures this beautifully in Philippians 2:5–8:

"Let this mind be in you which was also in Christ Jesus, who, being in the form of God, did not consider equality with God something to be used to His own advantage; rather, He made Himself nothing by taking the very nature of a servant."

Christ—the One worthy of all worship—modeled the ultimate form of worship by stooping low. His humility was not weakness; it was strength under submission. Every miracle He performed, every word He spoke, and every act of love flowed from a heart that honored the Father. In His life, worship was not confined to the synagogue or the Mount of Olives; it was lived daily in dusty streets, at dinner tables, and among sinners.

In the same way, our workplaces, classrooms, and homes become sanctuaries when our hearts carry the fragrance of gratitude, humility, and servanthood. These are the marks of a true worshipper in the marketplace.

Gratitude: The Language of Worship

Paul exhorts in 1 Thessalonians 5:18, *"In everything give thanks; for this is the will of God in Christ Jesus for you."*

Gratitude is not a reaction; it's a revelation. It shifts our focus from what is missing to what has been mercifully given. It transforms ordinary moments into sacred encounters. A grateful heart doesn't wait for everything to be perfect—it worships in the middle of imperfection.

Old Testament Example: Ruth's Grateful Spirit

Ruth's life paints a moving portrait of gratitude and humility. Though she lost her husband and left her homeland, she never complained or grew bitter. In Bethlehem, she chose to glean leftovers in the fields with a thankful heart. When Boaz noticed her, it wasn't her beauty that stood out—it was her humility and gratitude. Her words in Ruth 2:10 echo the tone of a true worshipper:

"Why have I found favor in your eyes, that you should take notice of me, a foreigner?"

Ruth's gratitude positioned her for divine favor. God delights in grateful hearts because gratitude magnifies His goodness, even in scarcity. Worshippers like Ruth turn fields of lack into altars of praise.

Modern Example: Meera, the Schoolteacher

Meera, a high school teacher, worked in a government school with limited resources and an unmotivated staff. Many of her colleagues complained daily about low salaries and poor management. But Meera decided to change her attitude. Each morning before class, she would whisper a prayer of thanks—thanking God for her students, her chalkboard, and even the noisy classroom.

Over time, her joy became contagious. Her students began to respond differently; they respected her and even tried harder. One of her fellow teachers once said, *"I don't know what Meera has, but whatever it is, it's more powerful than any salary increment."*

What Meera carried was worship—expressed through gratitude. She had turned her classroom into her temple, and her lessons into offerings.

Gratitude sanctifies the space we occupy. It transforms our perspective and invites God's presence into our daily routine.

Humility: The Posture of the Worshipper

Humility is not thinking less of yourself—it's thinking of yourself less. It's living with an awareness that everything we have and are is by the grace of God. Worship and pride cannot coexist; one will always drive out the other.

The Bible says in James 4:6,

"God resists the proud but gives grace to the humble."

Old Testament Example: Ruth and David

We see humility exemplified again in Ruth's story and also in David's life. David, though anointed as king, never demanded the throne. He served Saul faithfully, even when Saul sought his life. His humility in waiting for God's timing revealed a worshipful heart.

David wrote in Psalm 131:1–2,

"My heart is not proud, Lord, my eyes are not haughty; I do not concern myself with great matters… but I have calmed and quieted myself."

A humble heart is a heart that worships quietly even when unseen.

New Testament Example: Jesus Washing Feet

In John 13, Jesus performed one of the most profound acts of humility: He washed His disciples' feet. The Master became the servant. When He finished, He said,

"I have set you an example that you should do as I have done for you." (John 13:15)

That moment wasn't just about clean feet—it was about clean hearts. Jesus was teaching that worship is not only about adoration but also about imitation. We worship Him best when we reflect His character.

Modern Example: Samuel, the Team Leader

Samuel worked as a team leader in a large IT firm. His team members often described him as "different." He never used his position to dominate but to serve. If a project deadline was tight, he would stay late, not to micromanage but to help. Once, when a junior developer made a costly error that could have jeopardized their client relationship, Samuel took responsibility before the management team. Later, when asked why he didn't expose the employee, he replied, "If Jesus could wash feet, I can cover a mistake."

His humility spoke louder than any sermon. Over time, his leadership transformed the culture of his team. Worship had found expression in humility.

Servanthood: Worship in Action

Servanthood is where gratitude and humility converge. It's worship in motion. To serve is to mirror the heart of Christ, who came “not to be served, but to serve” (Matthew 20:28).

True servanthood doesn't require a platform; it thrives in the unseen corners of life—when you help a colleague without recognition, when you give your best even when no one notices, when you choose to bless rather than complain.

Biblical Example: Jesus, the Servant King

Jesus' entire ministry was a symphony of servanthood. From healing the sick to feeding the hungry, His every act revealed the heart of the Father. He served because He loved, and He loved because He worshipped.

Modern Example: Ramesh, the Manager Who Served

Ramesh was a mid-level manager in a logistics company. When his department faced layoffs, he made an unusual choice. Instead of protecting his position, he advocated for his team. He personally trained them in new roles so they could be retained in other departments. One day, a colleague asked, “Why do you care so much? Most managers would protect themselves.”

Ramesh smiled and replied, “Because my boss is not in this office—He's in heaven. I'm just serving Him through my people.”

That's what worship in the marketplace looks like—when servanthood becomes your leadership style.

Turning Complaints into Worshipful Gratitude

Every day offers two choices: to complain or to worship. Complaining magnifies problems; worship magnifies God. The Israelites' journey in the wilderness reveals this truth vividly. Their complaints delayed their destiny. Gratitude, on the other hand, draws God's favor and presence.

A practical way to cultivate this is through a Gratitude Journal. Each morning, list three things you are thankful for at work—colleagues, opportunities, even challenges. Over time, you'll see how gratitude shifts not just your emotions but your environment.

A Worshipper's Declaration

"Lord, I thank You for this day, this work, and these people You've placed around me. Help me to serve with humility, to work with gratitude, and to lead with love. Let my words, my attitude, and my actions rise before You as worship. Teach me to find You not only in the sanctuary but in every spreadsheet, classroom, and corridor. May my workplace become an altar where Your glory is revealed."

Key Takeaway

Worship is not a song we sing but a life we live. Gratitude keeps our heart pure, humility keeps our spirit tender, and servanthood keeps our focus right. When these attitudes blend, heaven touches earth—even in boardrooms, classrooms, and coffee shops.

When we live this way, every task—big or small—becomes sacred. And as we serve with thankful hearts, we discover that the truest form of worship is not found in lifting our hands, but in bending our knees.

Chapter 6:
Worship through Relationships – Loving People on Purpose

Worship is not only the sound that rises from our lips but also the love that flows from our lives. True worship doesn't end when the song stops—it continues in how we treat people. If our voices rise in praise on Sunday but our words tear others down on Monday, we have missed the heart of worship. Jesus made this unmistakably clear when He said,
"By this all men will know you are My disciples, if you love one another." (John 13:35)
The measure of our worship is not merely in the melodies we sing, but in the mercy we show. The world doesn't need more eloquent preachers or perfect worship sets—it needs believers whose relationships reflect the heart of God.

Love: The True Language of Worship
In **Romans 12:10**, Paul exhorts, *"Be devoted to one another in love. Honor one another above yourselves."*
Love is the highest form of worship because it is the nature of God Himself. When we love intentionally, we bring His character into our workplaces, families, and communities. Worship is not confined to what we offer God directly—it's also revealed in how we treat those made in His image.
The marketplace, with its competition, deadlines, and pressures, often tests this love the most. But it is in these very places that worship through relationships shines brightest.

Old Testament Example: Jonathan and David – The Covenant of Loyal Love

The friendship between Jonathan and David in the Old Testament offers one of the purest pictures of love and loyalty in Scripture. Jonathan, the son of King Saul, had every reason to see David as a rival—David was the rising star of Israel, the one who had slain Goliath and captured the nation's heart. Yet instead of jealousy, Jonathan chose love.

In 1 Samuel 18:3–4, it says, *"Then Jonathan made a covenant with David, because he loved him as his own soul. And Jonathan took off the robe that was on him and gave it to David."*

That robe symbolized royalty and inheritance—everything Jonathan could have claimed for himself. Yet he willingly laid it down to honor what God was doing through David. His friendship was not built on convenience but on covenant.

Jonathan's love was an act of worship. He recognized God's hand upon David and chose to serve God's purpose above his own ambition. It was love in action—costly, intentional, and selfless.

New Testament Example: Jesus and His Disciples – Love Beyond Comfort

Jesus' relationship with His disciples was equally instructive. They were flawed, inconsistent, and often misunderstood His mission, yet He loved them to the end (John 13:1). When He washed their feet, including Judas's—the one who would betray Him—He was not performing a ritual but demonstrating relational worship.

In that moment, Jesus showed us that worship is not about status but service. It's about loving those who least deserve it because that's what God did for us.
When we love the difficult colleague, forgive the unfair boss, or encourage the discouraged coworker, we are not merely being kind—we are worshipping God in the truest sense.

Modern Example: Anaya, the College Student Who Chose Love

Anaya was in her second year of college—bright, friendly, and involved in her church youth group. But on campus, she often noticed a student named Arjun who sat alone in the cafeteria. Rumors had spread that he was "weird" because he didn't talk much and preferred sketching in his notebook during breaks. Most avoided him.
One afternoon, Anaya felt a quiet nudge in her spirit. She took her lunch tray and sat across from him. The first few days were awkward; he barely spoke. But she kept showing up—with a smile, a kind word, sometimes a shared snack. Gradually, Arjun began to open up. She discovered he had recently lost his father and struggled with anxiety. Her simple act of intentional love became the doorway to healing in his life.
Months later, Arjun told her, *"You were the first person who made me feel seen. I used to think God forgot about me, but you reminded me He hadn't."*
Anaya didn't preach a sermon—she lived one. Her consistency, kindness, and patience became an offering of worship to God. Loving people intentionally transforms ordinary relationships into sacred ground.

Worship in the Marketplace: Loving When It's Difficult

It's easy to love those who are lovable, but worship through relationships is tested when love requires effort. In every office, classroom, or home, there will always be a "Saul" to our "David"—someone who tests our patience or misunderstands our motives. But remember what Jesus said in Matthew 5:44,

"Love your enemies and pray for those who persecute you."

This kind of love is supernatural. It cannot be manufactured; it must be cultivated through the Spirit. When we respond to rudeness with grace or to criticism with kindness, we are offering a fragrance of worship that heaven recognizes.

Forgiveness: The Fragrance of True Worship

Unforgiveness is one of the greatest barriers to worship. It clogs the spiritual arteries of our soul. Jesus said in Matthew 6:14–15,

"If you forgive others their trespasses, your heavenly Father will also forgive you."

When we forgive, we imitate God's greatest act of mercy. Worship is never complete without forgiveness, because love and bitterness cannot coexist in the same heart.

Example: Marcus, the Sales Executive

Marcus worked as a senior sales executive in a competitive firm. A colleague once betrayed him by taking credit for a deal he had spent months cultivating. The injustice ate at him. Every Sunday, he would lift his hands in church, but inside, he carried resentment.

One day, during prayer, the Holy Spirit gently reminded him of Jesus' words: *"Forgive, as I have forgiven you."* It wasn't easy. But Marcus made the decision to forgive his colleague and even began praying for his success.

In time, that act of forgiveness freed Marcus—not only emotionally but spiritually. His joy returned, his work flourished, and his witness deepened. His boss once remarked, *"There's something different about you now—you seem lighter."* Marcus smiled and said, "That's what happens when you let go and worship God through forgiveness."

Forgiveness is the incense of relational worship—it rises silently but powerfully before God.

Practical Application: The Relational Worship Audit

Worship through relationships is not accidental—it's intentional. It requires reflection and realignment. Take a moment to evaluate your relationships using this "Relational Worship Audit."

Ask yourself:

- ✓ **Love** – Am I genuinely loving the people God has placed around me, or merely tolerating them?
- ✓ **Forgiveness** – Is there anyone I'm still holding a grudge against?
- ✓ **Encouragement** – Do my words build others up or tear them down?
- ✓ **Service** – Have I looked for ways to serve someone this week without expecting anything in return?
- ✓ **Witness** – Can others sense God's presence through the way I treat them?

Worship thrives when relationships are healthy. The more we love, forgive, and serve, the stronger our witness becomes in the marketplace.

Reflection Exercise: Loving on Purpose

At the end of each day this week, take five minutes to reflect:

- ✓ *Whom did I love today on purpose?*
- ✓ *Whom did I struggle to love, and why?*
- ✓ *What would Jesus have done differently in that interaction?*

Then pray:

"Lord, teach me to love like You do. Let my words be gentle, my actions kind, and my heart forgiving. Help me to see every person as someone You died for. Make my relationships a reflection of Your love."

Key Takeaway

Worship through relationships is the most visible form of our devotion. It's how the world recognizes that we belong to Jesus—not by our songs, sermons, or symbols, but by our love. Every conversation becomes an opportunity for adoration. Every act of kindness becomes a chorus of praise.

When love governs our interactions, the office becomes a sanctuary, the classroom a cathedral, and every handshake a holy moment.

To worship God is to love people on purpose—and when we do, heaven takes notice.

Chapter 7:
Worship through Adversity – Praising God in the Pressure Cooker

Worship is easy when life is smooth, when prayers are answered quickly, and when the sun is shining. But the truest test of worship comes not in moments of comfort, but in seasons of conflict. It's in the pressure cooker of adversity that the authenticity of our worship is revealed. Anyone can sing when life is good, but only a true worshipper sings in the storm.

Adversity refines our faith like fire purifies gold. It removes the impurities of self-reliance, pride, and shallow praise, leaving behind a heart that worships God not for what He gives, but for who He is.

Praising in the Pain

The Apostle Paul captured this paradox beautifully in 1 Thessalonians 5:18:

"Give thanks in all circumstances; for this is God's will for you in Christ Jesus."

Notice Paul didn't say *for* all circumstances, but *in* all circumstances. We are not called to thank God for pain, betrayal, or loss—but to worship Him in the midst of them, because He remains faithful even when life is not.

Worship in adversity declares to the world—and to our own souls—that our God is bigger than our battle. It shifts the atmosphere from despair to hope and transforms our perspective from *"Why me?"* to *"What are You teaching me, Lord?"*

Old Testament Example: Job – Worship When It Hurts

Few lives capture this truth better than Job's. In a single day, he lost everything—his wealth, his children, his health, and his peace. Yet in the face of unimaginable pain, Job's response was one of worship: *"Then Job arose, tore his robe, shaved his head, and fell to the ground and worshiped. And he said, 'The Lord gave, and the Lord has taken away; blessed be the name of the Lord.'"* (Job 1:20–21)

Job's worship didn't come from a place of denial, but of deep surrender. He wept, he questioned, he wrestled—but he never abandoned his reverence for God. His worship was raw and real, not polished or perfect.

In the end, God restored Job's fortunes—not because Job endured flawlessly, but because he refused to let his pain silence his praise. Job teaches us that true worship is not conditional; it's covenantal. It's not built on outcomes but on relationship.

New Testament Example: Paul and Silas – Songs in the Midnight Hour

Fast forward to the New Testament, and we find Paul and Silas in another pressure cooker moment. They had obeyed God's call to preach in Philippi, yet found themselves beaten and imprisoned unjustly. Most people would have complained or questioned God's goodness—but not these two.

Acts 16:25 records,*"About midnight Paul and Silas were praying and singing hymns to God, and the other prisoners were listening to them."*

Their worship became the key to their deliverance. The prison doors swung open, chains fell off, and

hearts were changed—not just theirs, but the jailer's as well.
Worship in adversity doesn't just set *you* free; it releases others too. When we choose praise over panic, heaven moves in ways we cannot imagine.

Modern Example: Nisha's Midnight Song

Nisha was a young entrepreneur who had poured everything into her small café. It wasn't just a business to her—it was her dream and ministry. She hired local youth, prayed over every seat, and even played soft worship music throughout the day. But when the pandemic hit, everything collapsed. With months of lockdown, bills piling up, and no customers, Nisha found herself on the edge of despair.
One night, she sat on the café floor surrounded by unpaid invoices and whispered, *"God, I don't understand why You let this happen."* Tears flowed freely. Then she heard a quiet whisper in her heart: *"Worship Me here."*
So she did. Her voice cracked as she began to sing *"Great is Thy Faithfulness."* The song echoed through the empty café—raw, trembling, but sincere. The next morning, something shifted. Peace replaced panic.
Though her situation didn't change overnight, doors slowly began to open. A local bakery offered to share their space; loyal customers started ordering online; even new investors came along months later. But Nisha knew the real miracle had already happened the night she chose to worship in her wilderness.
Worship doesn't always change our circumstances immediately—but it always changes *us*.

The Refining Fire: What Adversity Produces
In the marketplace, adversity can come in many forms—a failed deal, a betrayal, an unfair boss, or a sudden loss. But these seasons can become sacred classrooms if we let them.
Romans 5:3–4 reminds us,
"We glory in our sufferings, because we know that suffering produces perseverance; perseverance, character; and character, hope."
Every challenge is an opportunity for worship because it reveals what we truly believe about God. Do we trust Him only when things go our way, or do we trust Him *because* He is God—even when we don't understand His ways?
When we worship in adversity:

- ✓ ***Faith deepens.*** *Our dependence shifts from resources to the Source.*
- ✓ ***Character strengthens.*** *We learn patience, humility, and compassion.*
- ✓ ***Witness grows.*** *People around us notice that our joy isn't circumstantial—it's supernatural.*

Like gold refined in the fire, adversity purifies our praise until only sincerity remains.

Old Testament Echo: The Three Hebrew Boys
Another powerful example of worship in adversity is found in Daniel 3. Shadrach, Meshach, and Abednego refused to bow to Nebuchadnezzar's golden idol. Their allegiance belonged only to God—even if it meant death.
Their words still ring through time:
"Our God whom we serve is able to deliver us... but even if He does not, we will not bow." (Daniel 3:17–18)
That's worship—unconditional, unshakable, unafraid.

God didn't keep them out of the fire; He met them in it. The same is true for us. In every fiery trial, there walks a Fourth Man—the Son of God—turning our flames into fellowship.

When Worship Breaks the Chains

Adversity can make us bitter or better, depending on what we focus on. The enemy wants to use hardship to silence your worship, but God uses it to strengthen your song.

When you praise God in the pressure cooker—when you choose faith over fear, surrender over striving—you are declaring that God is greater than your storm.

That kind of worship confuses the enemy and compels heaven. The chains that held you—fear, anxiety, despair—begin to fall. You find yourself freer than before, even if your circumstances haven't yet changed.

Practical Application: Building an Altar in the Storm

When adversity strikes, build an altar—not of complaint, but of worship. Here's how:

- ✓ *Acknowledge the pain honestly. God is not offended by your tears.*
- ✓ *Affirm His character. Say aloud who He is, even when your emotions waver.*
- ✓ *Activate gratitude. List three things you can still thank Him for.*
- ✓ *Align your heart through song or prayer. Even a whisper of worship shifts the atmosphere.*

Remember what Habakkuk declared in the midst of national collapse: "*Though the fig tree does not blossom... yet I will rejoice in the Lord."* (Habakkuk 3:17–18)

That's worship in its purest form—praise that rises even from the ashes.

Modern Reflection: The Workplace Pressure Cooker

Consider Arvind, a mid-level project manager who faced public criticism after a failed project. Though the failure wasn't entirely his fault, the burden of blame crushed him. He could have lashed out or withdrawn in shame—but instead, he prayed every morning before stepping into the office: "Lord, help me worship You with how I respond today."

He chose grace over grumbling, served his team faithfully, and refused to defend himself in pride. Months later, when the truth surfaced, his integrity became evident, and he was promoted—not just in title, but in testimony.

Arvind's story reminds us that sometimes the real miracle isn't deliverance *from* the fire, but endurance *in* it.

Reflection Exercise: Praise Under Pressure

Take a quiet moment and reflect:

- ✓ *What current adversity am I facing that feels like a prison or furnace?*
- ✓ *How can I choose worship instead of worry today?*
- ✓ *What would it look like to sing my way through this season?*

Then write a short "midnight song"—a few lines declaring your trust in God, even in the darkness. Keep it on your phone or desk. When the pressure rises, sing it as your personal act of defiance against fear.

Closing Prayer

"Father, even in my fire, You are faithful.
When I don't understand, help me still to worship.
Let my pain become praise, my tears become testimony,
And my pressure become the place where Your presence is revealed.
Teach me to sing at midnight, to trust when I can't trace,
And to remember that You are always worthy."

Key Takeaway

Worship in adversity is not denial of reality—it's declaration of divine sovereignty. It says, *"My circumstances may change, but my God never will."*

When we learn to praise in the pressure cooker, the fire no longer burns us—it refines us. The prison no longer confines us—it becomes our platform.

In the end, adversity doesn't silence the true worshipper—it gives them a new song.

Chapter 8:
Overcoming the Babylon System – Standing Firm in a Corrupt World

The world we live in today is not very different from the Babylon that Daniel and his friends faced. It is sophisticated, seductive, and systemically opposed to the values of God. Babylon represents more than a geographical kingdom—it symbolizes a mindset, a system that prioritizes self-glory over God's glory, wealth over worship, and compromise over conviction. It whispers, *"Bow down just this once, and you'll fit in."* But God is still looking for those who, like Daniel, Shadrach, Meshach, and Abednego, will stand firm even when the world says, *"Everyone is doing it."*

The Call to Stand in a Conforming Culture

Romans 12:2 declares, *"Do not be conformed to this world, but be transformed by the renewing of your mind."* Paul's call is as relevant now as it was then. The word *"conform"* literally means to be pressed into a mold—to take the shape of whatever environment surrounds you. The Babylon system tries to mold believers into its image through peer pressure, workplace expectations, moral compromises, and the relentless pursuit of success at any cost.

But those who have encountered the Living God understand that worship is not just about singing songs on Sunday—it's about whom you *bow to* from Monday to Saturday. Worship is allegiance, and allegiance demands loyalty even when it costs us something.

The Test of the Furnace

Daniel 3 gives us one of the most compelling pictures of uncompromising worship. King Nebuchadnezzar builds a golden statue ninety feet high and commands everyone to bow down at the sound of the music. For Shadrach, Meshach, and Abednego, it was more than a public display—it was a test of loyalty.

Their answer still echoes across generations:

"O Nebuchadnezzar, we do not need to defend ourselves before you in this matter. If we are thrown into the blazing furnace, the God we serve is able to deliver us… But even if He does not, we want you to know, O king, that we will not serve your gods or worship the image of gold you have set up." – Daniel 3:16–18

Their worship was not dependent on the outcome but on their conviction. They knew that *true worshippers don't bow to circumstances—they bow to Christ.*

God didn't prevent them from being thrown into the fire, but He joined them in it. The Bible records that the king saw *"four men walking in the fire, unbound and unharmed"* (Daniel 3:25). This is the secret of overcoming Babylon—you don't stand alone; you stand with Him.

Esther's Silent Strength

Centuries later, another worshipper faced her own Babylon. Esther, a young Jewish girl turned queen in Persia, was confronted with a defining choice—to remain silent or to risk her life for her people. Her cousin Mordecai's words cut through her fear:

"Who knows but that you have come to your royal position for such a time as this?" – Esther 4:14

Esther's courage was not displayed in public worship or prophetic declarations but in quiet obedience and sacrificial resolve. She fasted, prayed, and then walked into the throne room knowing her life could end with one wrong move. Her act of worship was her willingness to stand for God's cause in a corrupt palace.

Esther teaches us that sometimes standing firm doesn't mean shouting louder—it means obeying God when silence is easier and safer.

Modern Babylon: The Pressure to Compromise

Meet Arvind, a senior government officer responsible for approving tenders for infrastructure projects. He had always been known for his efficiency and professionalism, but one day a lucrative offer came his way—a contractor promised him a sizable "gift" in return for a favorable decision. The system expected it; his colleagues shrugged it off as "normal."

Arvind wrestled with the decision. On one hand, his children's college expenses loomed large. On the other, his conscience reminded him that no amount of comfort could buy back integrity once sold. Late one night, he read *Proverbs 11:1*: *"Dishonest scales are detestable to the Lord, but accurate weights find favor with Him."*

The next morning, he declined the offer and approved the tender purely on merit. Within months, he was transferred to a less glamorous posting. Yet, though the move felt like a setback, Arvind testified later that it was the most peaceful season of his life. His quiet refusal to bow became an act of worship, an offering of integrity that rose like incense before God.

Standing Firm in Today's World

Standing firm in today's Babylon may not mean facing fiery furnaces or royal decrees, but it does mean refusing to bend the knee to greed, gossip, immorality, or deceit. It may mean being the only one in the meeting who says, *"This isn't right."* It may mean losing a deal, declining a promotion, or walking away from a friendship that corrupts your convictions. But remember, God honors those who honor Him (1 Samuel 2:30). The stand you take today becomes the seed for God's favor tomorrow.

Reflection: Where Do I Bow Unknowingly?

Before we point fingers at the obvious idols in our culture, we must ask ourselves:

- ✓ *Where do I bow unknowingly?*
- ✓ Do I bow to approval, seeking validation more than God's voice?
- ✓ Do I bow to ambition, chasing success at the cost of peace and purity?
- ✓ Do I bow to comfort, avoiding confrontation even when truth is at stake?

Babylon doesn't always demand an outward bow; sometimes it wins through inward compromise. But worshippers called to influence the marketplace must learn to discern these subtle forms of idolatry.

Setting Spiritual Boundaries

To thrive in Babylon without becoming Babylon, you must set clear spiritual boundaries. Daniel refused to eat the king's food (Daniel 1:8), not out of rebellion, but conviction. His decision preserved his purity and testimony. Similarly, we must draw our own lines—boundaries in speech, relationships, finances, and decisions.

Here are a few practical principles to build those boundaries:

- ✓ *Accountability: Have a trusted spiritual friend or mentor who can ask you the hard questions.*
- ✓ *Prayer and the Word: Daniel prayed three times a day even when it was outlawed (Daniel 6:10). Prayer keeps your heart aligned when the world tries to twist it.*
- ✓ *Purpose: Know why you are where you are. You are not in that company, school, or government office by accident—you are God's ambassador there.*

The Reward of the Uncompromising

God didn't just deliver the three Hebrews; He promoted them. Daniel 3:30 records, *"Then the king promoted Shadrach, Meshach, and Abednego in the province of Babylon."* When you refuse to bow, God causes kings to take notice. The world respects integrity even when it resists it.

In the end, Babylon will fall—as Revelation 18 declares—but those who stand for God will reign with Him.

Closing Thought:

To overcome Babylon is to worship without compromise. Every act of resistance against corruption, every "no" to temptation, and every moment of truthfulness in the dark is an act of worship. It's declaring to heaven and earth: *"My allegiance is to the King of kings."*

And when the flames rise, may it be said of us as it was of those three Hebrew men—*"They trusted in their God… and yielded their bodies, that they might not serve nor worship any god except their own God."* (Daniel 3:28)

Chapter 9: Money, Motives & Marketplace Worship

True Prosperity Glorifies God, Not Self

Money. Few things in life test the heart of a worshipper more. It promises security, comfort, and status—but it also exposes what we truly value. The marketplace runs on transactions, numbers, and profit margins, yet beneath it all lies a deeper spiritual truth: money is not just a currency; it is a revealer of worship.

Jesus made this uncomfortably clear when He said in *Matthew 6:24*, *"No one can serve two masters. Either you will hate the one and love the other… You cannot serve both God and mammon."* Notice that He did not say we *should not* serve both—He said we *cannot.* The human heart is not wired to worship two masters. One will always take the throne.

Money itself is not evil—Scripture never said that. It is *the love of money* that becomes *"the root of all kinds of evil"* (*1 Timothy 6:10*). In the hands of a worshipper, money becomes a tool to glorify God; in the hands of an idolater, it becomes a snare that destroys purpose. The question is not whether you have money, but whether money has you.

The Blessing and the Test of Prosperity

When Moses warned Israel in *Deuteronomy 8:17–18*, he was addressing a very human danger: the pride that prosperity brings.

"You may say to yourself, 'My power and the strength of my hands have produced this wealth for me.' But

remember the Lord your God, for it is He who gives you power to get wealth, and so confirms His covenant."

The ability to create, manage, and multiply wealth is a divine gift. But it is also a divine test. Every paycheck, every business deal, and every investment carries a quiet question from heaven: *Will you remember who the Source is?*

Solomon: Wisdom, Wealth, and a Wandering Heart

No one embodied the paradox of wealth and worship quite like Solomon. His early reign shone with humility and devotion. When God appeared to him in a dream and offered anything he desired, Solomon didn't ask for riches or power; he asked for wisdom to lead God's people well (*1 Kings 3:9*). God was so pleased that He gave Solomon both wisdom *and* wealth.

At his peak, Solomon's prosperity was unmatched—gold flowed into his treasury, his ships brought exotic goods from distant lands, and kings sought his counsel. The Bible records that silver was *"as common as stones in Jerusalem"* (*1 Kings 10:27*).

But somewhere along the way, the worshipper became the worshipped. His wealth and influence seduced him into alliances with pagan nations. He built altars for foreign gods and allowed his heart to be divided. His downfall wasn't sudden; it was subtle—a slow drift from gratitude to greed, from worshipping the Giver to admiring the gifts.

Solomon's life stands as both a model and a warning: **Wisdom brings wealth, but only worship keeps it holy.**

The Modern Marketplace: The Silent Idol

Consider Neha, a young entrepreneur in Mumbai who started a small design studio with nothing but her laptop and faith. Her work ethic and creativity soon earned her major clients, and before long, the business took off. As her income grew, so did the temptation to live for more—more prestige, more possessions, more applause.

One Sunday, during worship, her pastor read *Matthew 6:19–21*:

"Do not store up for yourselves treasures on earth... but store up treasures in heaven. For where your treasure is, there your heart will be also."

That verse pierced her like an arrow. Neha realized she had begun to find her identity not in being a child of God, but in being a "successful entrepreneur." She had built a brand, but she was losing her balance.

The next week, she made a quiet decision—she would dedicate a portion of her profits to fund kingdom projects: children's education, missions, and church community programs. Over time, her business became not just a source of income but an altar of impact. Her office became a place of prayer; her profits became her offering.

In doing so, Neha discovered something powerful: *Money is safest when it's surrendered.*

Jesus and the Heart of Giving

Throughout the New Testament, Jesus consistently linked worship with generosity. When He watched people giving in the temple, He didn't commend the rich who gave large sums, but a widow who offered two copper coins—all she had (*Mark 12:41–44*). Heaven's measure of giving is never about the amount—it's about the motive.

In *Luke 16:10–11*, Jesus said, *"Whoever can be trusted with very little can also be trusted with much… So if you have not been trustworthy in handling worldly wealth, who will trust you with true riches?"*

The principle is clear: How we handle money determines what spiritual authority we can carry. Faithfulness in finances is not separate from worship—it *is* worship.

Money and Motive: The Invisible Battle

In the marketplace, motives are often hidden behind polished smiles and professional contracts. But God looks deeper. He isn't impressed by how much we earn; He is interested in why we earn.

Two employees can do the same job—one works to glorify God, the other to glorify self—and heaven records them differently.

Money is an amplifier—it magnifies what already exists in the heart. If you are generous, more money will make you more generous. If you are self-centered, more money will only deepen your selfishness.

This is why Jesus' command to *"seek first the kingdom of God"* (*Matthew 6:33*) is so vital. When the Kingdom is the priority, money becomes the servant, not the master.

True Prosperity: A Kingdom Perspective

Biblical prosperity is not measured by the size of your bank account, but by the impact of your obedience. Abraham was wealthy, yet his heart remained free—he was willing to offer Isaac, the very promise God gave him. Job lost everything but never cursed God. Lydia, a businesswoman in the New Testament (*Acts*

16:14–15), used her success to open her home for the church.

True prosperity is having enough to fulfill God's purpose for your life and bless others in the process. It's about stewardship, not ownership. We are not called to hoard; we are called to *channel.*

The Worshipper's Wallet: Stewardship in Action

When our hearts are surrendered, our finances follow. Managing money becomes a sacred act of worship—tithing, giving, saving, budgeting, investing—all under the Lordship of Christ.

Stewardship is not about how much you give; it's about how faithfully you handle what's been given. A worshipper doesn't say, *"How much of my money should I give to God?" but rather, "How much of God's money should I keep for my needs?"*

Proverbs 3:9–10 reminds us, *"Honor the Lord with your wealth, with the firstfruits of all your crops; then your barns will be filled to overflowing."*

When you place God first, He multiplies what remains.

A Personal Reflection

Ask yourself:

- ✓ *Do I see money as a master, a measure, or a means?*
- ✓ *Do I define success by what I accumulate or by how I contribute?*
- ✓ *If God asked for everything today, could I let it go without resentment?*

The answers to these questions reveal whether you serve God or mammon.

The Power of a Redeemed Motive

When Neha later shared her testimony at a business gathering, she said something that left the audience silent:

"The moment I stopped chasing money, it started following me—but more importantly, it started following God's purpose."

Her statement summarized a profound truth: God doesn't mind blessing you with wealth—as long as wealth doesn't blind you to Him.

In the kingdom, prosperity is never an end; it's always a means. The ultimate test of worship is not how loudly you sing, but how loosely you hold.

Closing Thought

Money is a good servant but a terrible master. It will either fuel your worship or fund your downfall. Every business decision, every paycheck, and every investment opportunity is a chance to declare whom you truly trust.

When your motives are pure, your work becomes your worship, your profit becomes your praise, and your prosperity becomes proof that God can trust you with His resources.

For it is He who gives you power to get wealth—so that His covenant may be established on the earth. (Deuteronomy 8:18)

Chapter 10: The Sound of Worship in the Streets – Evangelism through Excellence

When most people hear the word *evangelism*, they think of preachers with microphones, gospel tracts, or door-to-door campaigns. While these are all powerful ways to share the Good News, there is another form of evangelism—one that doesn't begin on a platform, but in the heart of a worshipper. It's the evangelism that happens when the aroma of genuine worship fills ordinary streets, workplaces, and homes.

This kind of witness cannot be manufactured; it is the natural overflow of a life that truly belongs to God. When worship becomes a lifestyle, *it spills over as light that cannot be hidden*.

As Jesus said in *Matthew 5:16*, *"Let your light so shine before men, that they may see your good works and glorify your Father in heaven."*

Notice that Jesus didn't say, *"Let them hear your words."* He said, *"Let them see your good works."* True worship produces visible fruit—excellence, integrity, compassion, and joy—that points others toward the Source.

Worship That Turns Heads

In the book of *Acts 16:25–34*, we find Paul and Silas in a Roman prison, beaten and shackled for preaching the gospel. Yet, instead of despairing, they began to worship. At midnight, their voices rose above the darkness—*songs of praise echoing through the cold stone walls.* The other prisoners listened, and heaven responded. Suddenly, the foundations shook, the doors flew open, and everyone's chains fell off.

But here's the miracle beyond the shaking: the jailer, seeing what had happened, fell before them and asked, "Sirs, what must I do to be saved?" Their worship had preached a sermon no words could match.

Paul and Silas did not hold a crusade or distribute tracts; they simply worshipped in adversity. Their joy in suffering revealed a God more powerful than pain, and that authenticity drew a man to faith.

This is the sound of worship in the streets—not just songs, but the resonance of lives lived with such excellence and faith that the world takes notice.

Lydia: The Marketplace Missionary

Among the many unsung heroes of the early church is Lydia, a successful businesswoman from Thyatira, mentioned in *Acts 16:14–15*. She was a dealer in purple cloth—a luxury trade that demanded both skill and integrity. Scripture calls her *"a worshipper of God."*

When she heard Paul preaching by the riverside, "the Lord opened her heart," and she believed. Her response was immediate and practical: she offered her home as the first gathering place for the church in Philippi. Lydia's wealth became a witness, and her business became a bridge for the gospel.

Through her hospitality and influence, the message spread beyond synagogue walls into living rooms, marketplaces, and trade routes. Lydia reminds us that evangelism is not reserved for missionaries; it belongs to anyone whose worship spills naturally into their world.

Worship that Works at Work

Meet Rakesh, a delivery boy working for a popular food delivery company in Bengaluru. His job was ordinary—riding through traffic, delivering parcels, and facing grumpy customers. But Rakesh carried something extraordinary in his spirit. Every day before leaving home, he prayed, *"Lord, help me deliver more than food today—help me deliver joy."*

He smiled, spoke kindly, and never complained even when customers were rude. Once, during a heavy downpour, he reached a customer's door completely drenched but still cheerful. "*Sir,*" he said, handing over the parcel, *"may your evening be as warm as your meal."* The customer, surprised by his words, started a conversation and discovered Rakesh's faith. Over time, their friendship grew, and one evening that same customer, depressed and suicidal, called Rakesh. Instead of brushing it off, Rakesh prayed with him over the phone. Weeks later, that man began attending a local church.

Rakesh never preached from a pulpit. He preached through punctuality, kindness, and joy. His life whispered the gospel louder than a megaphone ever could.

Excellence as an Evangelistic Tool

There is something deeply spiritual about doing your work well. *Colossians 3:23–24* says, *"Whatever you do, work at it with all your heart, as working for the Lord, not for men... It is the Lord Christ you are serving."*

When you serve your clients, teach your students, clean your surroundings, or design a project with excellence, heaven notices. Excellence attracts attention—and when that excellence is married to humility and love, it opens doors for witness.

Consider Daniel in Babylon again (*Daniel 6:3*): *"Then this Daniel distinguished himself... because an excellent spirit was in him."* That "excellent spirit" made kings listen to him, not just because he was brilliant, but because his brilliance reflected his belief. Excellence became his evangelism.

Mediocrity never glorifies God. Sloppy work and careless attitudes dull the light of our witness. But excellence shines—it compels people to ask, *"What makes you different?"* And in that moment, your worship becomes your testimony.

When Worship Walks the Streets

In the New Testament, evangelism wasn't confined to sermons—it was believers living out their faith in public spaces. Acts records that they "broke bread from house to house," lived joyfully, and *"had favor with all the people."* The Lord added to their number daily, not because of events, but because of example.

In today's world, that might look like a teacher who prays for her students, a nurse who treats patients as image-bearers of God, or a banker who refuses dishonest gain. Worship in the streets looks like *faithfulness in the small things.*

The Quiet Power of Consistent Character

Another story comes from Anjali, a project coordinator in a multinational company. She was known for her calm spirit and commitment to integrity. When her manager once pressured her to manipulate numbers in a report to please a client,

she respectfully refused. It cost her a promotion, but over time, her honesty began to influence others.
Months later, a colleague going through a personal crisis came to her and said, *"You live differently. You don't gossip, you don't cut corners... what gives you such peace?"*
Anjali smiled and said, *"It's not me—it's Christ in me."*
That simple answer opened a door for discipleship. Her consistency had been preaching long before her words did.

The Gospel of Everyday Excellence
There's a phrase that captures this truth well: *"Preach the gospel at all times; if necessary, use words."* While spoken words matter, our lives speak first. Every act of kindness, every honest decision, every gracious response is a note in heaven's symphony of worship.
When you show up early, deliver quality work, honor others, and maintain joy under pressure—you are evangelizing. People might never step into your church, but they will step into your presence. And if your presence carries His presence, then your street becomes your sanctuary.
The goal is not to perform for approval but to live in such a way that your excellence, humility, and compassion point unmistakably to Christ.

The Witness of Worship
Acts 4:13 describes the moment when people saw the courage of Peter and John and "recognized that they had been with Jesus." That is what true worship does—it leaves traces of God's presence on a person's life.

Imagine a world where teachers teach, drivers drive, engineers build, and executives lead with such excellence that people *"recognize they have been with Jesus."* That's evangelism through worship. That's revival in the streets.

A Call to Let Worship Spill Over

Worship was never meant to end with raised hands—it begins there but flows outward in open hands that serve, bless, and uplift. Your workplace, your school, your neighborhood—they are your mission field. You may never know who is watching, but someone is.

As Paul wrote, *"We are a letter from Christ… known and read by everyone."* (*2 Corinthians 3:3*)

Your life is God's letter to the world. Let it be written in excellence, sealed in love, and delivered with joy.

Closing Thought

The sound of worship in the streets isn't the echo of instruments—it's the melody of transformed lives. It's the smile that disarms anger, the diligence that defies laziness, the forgiveness that silences revenge.

When we live as worshippers beyond the walls, our excellence becomes our evangelism, our kindness becomes our sermon, and our lives become the stage where God's glory is displayed.

So go ahead—*let your light so shine before men, that they may see your good works and glorify your Father in heaven. (Matthew 5:16)*

Street Worship Toolkit

Living the Sound of Worship in the Streets

Worship in the marketplace does not need a pulpit or a platform. It simply needs a willing heart that reflects the character of Christ in the ordinary. This "Street Worship Toolkit" is designed to help you practice daily excellence, integrity, and witness — not through noise, but through a *life that sings.*

1. Excellence Reflection Sheet

Use this short reflection each evening to evaluate how well your *worship at work* shone that day. It's not about guilt — it's about growth.

Reflection Prompts:

- ✓ *Did I give my best effort today, or did I settle for "good enough"?*
- ✓ *Was there a moment when I could have gone the extra mile but didn't? What stopped me?*
- ✓ *Did my work reflect the creativity and excellence of my Creator (Colossians 3:23)?*
- ✓ *Did I treat deadlines, tasks, and clients as if I were serving Jesus Himself?*
- ✓ *What can I do differently tomorrow to reflect His glory more clearly?*

At the end of this reflection, whisper a prayer:

"Lord, I offer my work today as worship. Teach me to serve You with excellence, not for applause but for Your glory."

2. Character-as-Witness Journal Prompts

Character is the most powerful microphone a believer can ever hold. Use these weekly journal questions to deepen your inner life — the soil from which your outward witness grows.

Journal Prompts:

- ✓ *When was the last time someone noticed something "different" about my attitude, honesty, or kindness? How did I respond?*
- ✓ *How do I handle criticism or correction? Do I react, or do I reflect Christ?*
- ✓ *What situations test my integrity most — and how can I invite God's strength into those moments?*
- ✓ *How do I speak about others behind their backs — especially colleagues or leaders?*
- ✓ *Who in my workplace, school, or community might need to see Jesus through my patience, joy, or forgiveness?*

Write these reflections prayerfully at the end of each week. They will help you cultivate a heart posture that *witnesses without words.*

3. Daily Streetlight Declaration

Every morning before you step out into the world — whether you're heading to the office, the classroom, the shop floor, or the street — declare this over your day:

"Father, today I go out as Your worshipper, not just Your worker. Let my hands be an extension of Your excellence, my words an echo of Your kindness, my attitude a mirror of Your humility, and my life a light that points others to You.

I refuse to blend in; I choose to shine. Make me Your streetlight — illuminating dark places with Your love and truth. In Jesus' name, Amen."

Repeat this declaration daily until it becomes second nature — until worship no longer feels like something you "go to," but something you *live out.*

4. Weekly Streetlight Challenge

Each week, pick one practical act that embodies *worship in the streets*:

- ✓ *Encourage a discouraged colleague with a sincere note.*
- ✓ *Stay late to help a teammate meet a deadline — without expecting credit.*
- ✓ *Pray silently for every person you interact with during the day.*
- ✓ *Choose gratitude instead of complaint when plans fall apart.*
- ✓ *Offer your skill or service to bless someone in need.*

At week's end, journal what you learned and how God used you. You'll begin to see how *ordinary actions* can become *extraordinary worship.*

Closing Thought:

"The loudest worship service might happen on a quiet street corner, in an honest boardroom, behind a grocery counter, or in the heart of one who refuses to bow to the world's noise."

When worship leaves the sanctuary and steps into the street, the world will hear the sound of heaven — not through sermons, but through the *lives of those who shine.*

Chapter 11:
The Worshipping Generation – Raising Kingdom Influencers

“Speak, Lord, Your servant is listening.”
– 1 Samuel 3:10
“Remember your Creator in the days of your youth.”
– Ecclesiastes 12:1

The sound of worship is not meant to fade with one generation and rise again with another. True worship — the kind that transforms nations and rebuilds broken walls — must be *taught, modeled, and passed down.*

Every great move of God begins with one generation teaching the next to value His presence above all else. Yet in today’s world, where ambition often overshadows calling and performance replaces purpose, the cry for a worshipping generation is louder than ever.

This chapter explores how we can raise children, students, and young professionals who do not just attend church but carry God’s presence into classrooms, boardrooms, campuses, and companies — a generation that doesn’t just sing about worship but *lives it.*

The Calling of Samuel – Hearing God Early

In 1 Samuel 3, the boy Samuel lay in the temple near the Ark of God. He wasn’t a priest yet, not even a prophet — just a young boy learning to serve. But one night, he heard a voice calling his name: *“Samuel, Samuel.”* Three times he mistook it for Eli’s voice until Eli, discerning the moment, instructed him,

"If He calls you again, say, 'Speak, Lord, your servant is listening.'"

That one response changed Samuel's life — and Israel's destiny.

From that day forward, the Bible says, *"The Lord was with Samuel as he grew up, and He let none of his words fall to the groun*d" (1 Samuel 3:19).

Notice that Samuel didn't hear God during a worship concert or festival. He heard God while *serving in the ordinary*. Worship begins where obedience meets listening. True worshippers are not found only in pulpits — they are being shaped in classrooms, offices, and quiet places of faithfulness.

If today's youth can learn to say *"Speak, Lord,"* in their studies, their choices, their careers, and their relationships, they will hear the same voice that raised prophets, kings, and reformers.

Daniel – A Worshipper in the Hall of Power

Daniel was likely a teenager when Babylon captured Jerusalem and carried him into exile. Stripped of his homeland, given a new name, and forced into a pagan education system, Daniel could have easily compromised his faith. But the Bible records something remarkable: *"Daniel purposed in his heart that he would not defile himself"* (Daniel 1:8).

That decision, made in his youth, set the tone for his entire life. When others bowed before the culture, Daniel stood firm before God. When others blended in, Daniel shone brightly. When others feared kings, Daniel honored the King of Kings.

His worship wasn't about singing hymns — it was about living holy in a hostile world. Because Daniel chose purity over popularity, God gave him wisdom and favor that made him ten times better than his peers (Daniel 1:20).

If our generation of youth learns that worship is not about a song but about a stand, we will see Daniels rising again — in government offices, tech companies, schools, and startups.

Jesus and His Disciples – The Model for Kingdom Mentorship

Jesus didn't go to seminaries to find His followers. He went to fishing boats, tax booths, and street corners. He called *young men* in the midst of their daily labor and turned them into apostles who would turn the world upside down (Acts 17:6).

He taught them how to pray, how to forgive, how to serve, and how to lead. They learned worship not in a temple choir, but by watching the Son of God wash their feet. Jesus' model of mentorship was relational and practical — He walked with them through real life.

This is the pattern the Church must recover. If we want to raise a worshipping generation, we must *walk with them* — not just preach to them. Worship cannot be caught from a distance; it must be modeled up close.

Modern Example: A Campus Awakening

In a small college in Bengaluru, a group of students began meeting during their lunch break in an unused classroom. Among them was Aaron, a second-year engineering student who had recently recommitted his life to Christ.

Aaron noticed that his campus was full of stress, comparison, and competition. Students cheated on exams, exaggerated resumes, and lived under the pressure to outperform one another. Instead of condemning, Aaron decided to quietly start something new.

He invited a few friends to pray once a week for their campus. They prayed for teachers, exams, and classmates. Within weeks, the group grew from five to twenty. Some who came were unbelievers drawn by the peace they felt. Soon, students started helping each other study, sharing meals, and even organizing clean-up drives.

By the time Aaron graduated, the atmosphere of the campus had changed. Their excellence and unity had become their evangelism. Professors began noticing the integrity of these students and calling them “the prayer group.”

Aaron’s story reminds us that revival often begins with responsibility — when a few decide that their studies, service, and speech can be acts of worship.

The Danger of Performance without Presence

Many young believers today are gifted, talented, and passionate — but passion without presence leads to burnout. Worship must never become performance-driven. When success becomes the goal instead of surrender, worship becomes hollow.

Solomon, the wisest man who ever lived, began as a worshipper. In 1 Kings 3, he offered a thousand burnt offerings to the Lord, and God appeared to him in a dream, granting him wisdom and wealth. But later in life, Solomon’s heart turned away from God as he sought pleasure and power (1 Kings 11:4). His downfall was not due to lack of intelligence but lack of intimacy.

We must teach this next generation that calling without communion is dangerous. Excellence is good. Achievement is honorable. But the presence of God is essential.

Raising a Worship Culture at Home and Church

Parents and mentors play a crucial role in shaping this worshipping generation. Eli almost missed Samuel's calling until he discerned the voice of God in that boy's life. In the same way, parents must learn to recognize and nurture the seeds of calling in their children.

Instead of asking*, "What do you want to be when you grow up?" we can ask, "What is God calling you to become for His Kingdom?"*

We must teach them to study with purpose, work with excellence, and lead with humility — *unto the Lord.*

Churches, too, must move beyond youth entertainment and toward youth empowerment. The goal is not to fill the pews with young people, but to fill the world with worshippers.

A worshipping generation doesn't just attend Sunday services — they bring service into Monday.

Modern Example: "The Innovators for Christ" Movement

In a bustling corporate hub in Pune, a young HR professional named Rina started a small after-hours fellowship with her colleagues. They would meet weekly to share how they could reflect Christ in their companies. Over time, they began mentoring college interns and visiting universities to conduct workshops on *Ethical Leadership and Faith at Work.*

Within three years, this small group became known as "The Innovators for Christ." They didn't carry banners or preach sermons, but they lived out a radical message: *Excellence is worship, and worship transforms culture.*

Through mentorship, prayer, and professional guidance, they influenced dozens of young professionals to see their careers not as ladders to climb but as platforms to serve. That's the power of one generation passing the flame to the next.

The Action Step: Kingdom Work Plans

One practical way to raise Kingdom influencers is by creating Kingdom Work Plans — simple, faith-driven roadmaps for how young people can turn their daily routines into worship.

A Kingdom Work Plan answers three questions:

- ✓ What has God gifted me with? (skills, studies, influence)
- ✓ How can I use it to serve others and glorify Him?
- ✓ What boundaries or disciplines will keep me aligned with His will?

When a young teacher writes, *"I will teach math as if I'm revealing the order of God's creation,"*
When a young doctor writes, "*I will treat every patient as a child of God,*"
When a young artist writes, *"I will create beauty that points to the Creator,"* — then worship leaves the stage and enters the street.

Each profession becomes a pulpit, each project an altar, and each moment a song.

Closing Reflection

The future of nations lies not merely in their economies or technologies but in the spiritual DNA of their next generation. If we raise children and youth who know how to worship God in the public square

— not just sing about Him in private — we will see transformation ripple through schools, offices, and governments.

This is God's dream — not just a church that gathers, but a generation that carries.

A generation that says, like Samuel, *"Speak, Lord, Your servant is listening."*

A generation that lives, like Daniel, *"I will not defile myself."*

A generation that declares, like Paul, *"For me to live is Christ."*

Let us raise not performers, but **presence carriers**.

Not influencers for self, but **Kingdom influencers** for Christ.

Not mere worship leaders on a platform, but worshippers in every profession.

For when the worshipping generation rises, the glory of the Lord will fill the earth — not just the church.

Kingdom Influencer Toolkit

Practical Tools to Raise and Live as Worshipping Influencers in Everyday Life

1. Youth Worship Declarations

Speak these daily to align your heart, habits, and purpose with the Kingdom.

1. **I am not defined by my grades, gifts, or goals — I am defined by God's grace.**
   (Ephesians 2:10 – "For we are His workmanship, created in Christ Jesus for good works.")
2. **My studies, work, and service are acts of worship to the Lord.**
   (Colossians 3:23 – "Whatever you do, work at it with all your heart, as working for the Lord.")
3. **I will pursue excellence, not for applause, but to honor the One who called me.**
   (Matthew 5:16 – "Let your light so shine before men…")
4. **I am an influencer of light, not a follower of trends.**
   (Romans 12:2 – "Do not conform to the pattern of this world.")
5. **My generation will not be lost to distraction — we will rise as worshippers in every field.**
   (Psalm 24:6 – "This is the generation of those who seek Him.")
6. **I carry the presence of God wherever I go — my classroom, my office, my city.**
   (Joshua 1:9 – "For the Lord your God is with you wherever you go.")

7. **I am a Kingdom builder, not a comfort seeker.**
   (Matthew 6:33 – "Seek first the Kingdom of God and His righteousness.")
8. **My success will glorify God, not me.**
   (Deuteronomy 8:18 – "It is He who gives you power to get wealth.")
9. **I will listen for God's voice in every decision I make.**
   (1 Samuel 3:10 – "Speak, Lord, Your servant is listening.")
10. **I live to make Jesus known — in word, work, and witness.**
   (Philippians 1:21 – "For me to live is Christ.")

Encourage youth groups, student fellowships, and young professionals to **declare these aloud each morning** — turning routine into revival.

2. Mentorship Reflection Sheet

Designed for mentors, parents, and leaders to guide the next generation intentionally.

Step 1: Observe

What unique talents or passions do you see in the person you're mentoring?

Example: Creative thinking, empathy, leadership, curiosity, persistence.

Step 2: Listen

What are they hearing or sensing God say about their calling?

Encourage them to journal moments when they feel stirred or burdened for a cause.

Step 3: Guide

Help them connect their skills to service.

Example: A gifted communicator can lead devotionals, a tech-savvy youth can help the church with media.

Step 4: Model

Remember, mentorship is not instruction alone — it's imitation.

Ask: "Am I living the kind of worshipful life I want them to learn from?"

Step 5: Pray Together

Close every session with prayer. Speak words of destiny over them.

"Lord, let their gifts glorify You, their choices reflect You, and their influence expand Your Kingdom."

(Scripture: 2 Timothy 2:2 – "What you have heard from me… entrust to faithful men who will be able to teach others also.")

Encourage mentors to revisit this sheet monthly, tracking both spiritual and personal growth.

3. Kingdom Work Plan Template

A simple yet powerful guide to turn your daily life into Kingdom-driven worship.

Name: ______________________________

Age/Profession/Field:

____

Date: ______________

1. My Calling Statement

What do I sense God is calling me to be or do?

"I believe God has called me to

______________________________ *to bring Him glory."*

2. My Worship in Action

How can I turn my work, study, or daily routine into an act of worship?

"I will glorify God in my
_____________________________ by
_____________________________."

Example: I will glorify God in my business by being honest, generous, and prayerful in every decision.

3. My Integrity Boundaries

Where am I most likely to face compromise, and how will I guard against it?

"When tempted to ____________________________,
I will choose ____________________________."

Example: When tempted to cheat in exams, I will trust God for grace and do my best.

4. My Growth Goals (Next 90 Days)

Spiritual Goals: ____________________________

Professional Goals:

____

Relationship Goals:

____

Example: Spend 15 minutes in prayer daily; improve punctuality; forgive my colleague.

5. Accountability Partner

Who will walk with me, encourage me, and pray with me through this journey?

Name: ____________________________

Contact: ____________________________

6. My Declaration:

"I am a Kingdom influencer. My work is worship, my words are witness, and my life is an offering. I will shine for Christ in every sphere He places me."

Final Word: The Flame Must Continue

This toolkit is not meant to be a checklist but a **living covenant** — a way to continually align heart, mind, and hands with the purpose of God. Each declaration, reflection, and plan becomes like a spark that keeps the fire of worship burning beyond the church walls.

When youth begin to plan their studies as worship, when professionals begin to lead meetings as ministry, when mentors begin to raise influencers instead of followers — *the Kingdom expands quietly, powerfully, and permanently.*

"And the earth shall be filled with the knowledge of the glory of the Lord as the waters cover the sea." — Habakkuk 2:14

Chapter 12: Worship in Seasons of Pressure and Pain

"The Lord gave, and the Lord has taken away; blessed be the name of the Lord." — *Job 1:21*
"About midnight Paul and Silas were praying and singing hymns to God, and the prisoners were listening to them." — *Acts 16:25*

Worship is easy when life feels predictable, when prayers are answered swiftly, and when everything we touch seems to prosper. But the truest worship is revealed not in the comfort of the sanctuary, but in the storm of suffering. It is when we choose to *bless God while bleeding* that heaven takes notice.

There comes a time in every believer's life — especially those called to live out their faith in the marketplace — when pressure intensifies, plans crumble, or injustice strikes. It may be a rejected promotion, a toxic boss, a failed business, or a season of silence from God. In those moments, worship shifts from melody to sacrifice. And it is there, in the crucible of pain, that the fragrance of true worship rises.

This chapter invites us to look closely at those who worshipped not because life was good, but because God still was.

Job: The Worshipper Who Refused Bitterness

Few stories in Scripture capture the collision between pain and praise like Job's. Job was a man who "*feared God and shunned evil*" (Job 1:1), a prosperous leader with wealth, influence, and family.

Yet in one devastating day, he lost everything — his possessions, his children, and his health.

In the ashes of his grief, Job fell to the ground, not in despair, but in worship:

"The Lord gave and the Lord has taken away; blessed be the name of the Lord." (Job 1:21)

Job's worship wasn't denial of pain — it was defiance against despair. He acknowledged the sovereignty of God even when his circumstances made no sense. The Bible records something extraordinary: *"In all this, Job did not sin by charging God with wrongdoing."* (Job 1:22)

This kind of worship is not born from songs but from surrender. It says, *"Even when I don't understand, I will trust."* Job's posture became a testimony to every suffering saint thereafter — that worship in pain is the highest form of faith.

David: The Worshipper in the Wilderness

Before David wore a crown, he bore a cave. Anointed to be king yet pursued by Saul, David spent years running from one desert to another. He had every reason to grow resentful — rejected by his leader, betrayed by his friends, and misunderstood by his family. Yet in those desolate places, David wrote psalms that continue to comfort millions.

"My soul is downcast within me; therefore I will remember You…" (Psalm 42:6)

"I will bless the Lord at all times; His praise shall continually be in my mouth." (Psalm 34:1)

It is striking that David didn't just worship when he sat on the throne — he worshipped when he hid in the cave. His harp resounded louder than his hardship.

Every psalm written in exile became proof that worship is not a reaction to life's comfort but a declaration of faith in life's chaos. In pain, David discovered what every believer must learn — that God is not absent in the wilderness; He is revealed there.

Paul and Silas: Worship that Breaks Chains

Centuries later, in a dark prison in Philippi, two weary missionaries lay chained to the floor. Their backs were torn from beatings, their mission seemed delayed, and their future uncertain. Yet around midnight, the prisoners heard something unexpected: singing.

"About midnight Paul and Silas were praying and singing hymns to God, and the prisoners were listening to them." (Acts 16:25)

They weren't worshipping for deliverance — they were worshipping because even in prison, God was still worthy. But heaven couldn't remain silent to such faith.

The next verse tells us, *"Suddenly there was a great earthquake... and everyone's chains were loosed."* (Acts 16:26)

Worship doesn't always change our situation immediately, but it always changes our spirit. And sometimes, like in that prison, it changes the atmosphere for everyone around us.

Modern Example: Grace, the Nurse Who Sang through Exhaustion

Grace had been a nurse for ten years at a city hospital, but nothing had prepared her for the global pandemic. Days blurred into nights. Shifts stretched endlessly. Fear hung thick in the corridors.

One morning, after a grueling twelve-hour shift, Grace walked into the hospital chapel, still in her PPE kit, and slumped to her knees. Tears streaked her tired face as she whispered, *"Lord, I'm empty. But You're still God."*

She didn't have words left to pray, so she began to hum softly — *"Great is Thy Faithfulness."* The melody cracked through her exhaustion like light through stained glass. Soon, other nurses began to stop by — some believers, some not. Together, they would sit for five minutes each day, breathing, weeping, and worshipping in silence.

Over the weeks, something shifted. The fear that had filled the ward began to lift. Colleagues who didn't believe started asking Grace to pray for their families. Her quiet worship had become a sanctuary for the weary.

When asked later how she managed to keep going, she smiled faintly and said,

"Worship became my oxygen when I couldn't breathe hope anymore."

Grace's story reminds us that sometimes worship doesn't roar — it whispers. It doesn't always sound victorious, but it remains faithful.

The Pressure of the Marketplace

In the modern workplace, pressure can take many forms — layoffs, deadlines, toxic culture, or ethical compromise. For many believers, the temptation is to separate their pain from their praise — to think God is only interested in our victories, not our valleys. Yet Scripture repeatedly shows that **our faith is tested not on the mountaintop but in the furnace**.

When you face injustice at work, when you feel overlooked or falsely accused, remember Joseph —

wrongly imprisoned but divinely positioned (Genesis 39:20-23). The Lord was *with* him even in the dungeon, turning the prison into preparation.

The worshipper's secret is this: pressure purifies, and pain produces praise that performance never can.

Maintaining a Heart of Worship under Pressure

Worship under pressure requires deliberate focus. It means shifting our attention from *what's happening to us* to *who is with us*. It means refusing to let our circumstances dictate our confession.

David said, *"Why, my soul, are you downcast? ... Put your hope in God, for I will yet praise Him."* (Psalm 42:5)

That phrase — *"I will yet praise Him"* — is the anthem of resilient worship.

It is the sound of a heart that chooses hope over despair. When we worship under pressure, we are declaring:

"My situation may not change today, but my God has not changed. And that's enough for me to praise Him."

This kind of worship shakes the unseen realm. It silences the enemy's accusations and aligns our spirit with heaven's truth.

Reflection: What Happens When You Worship in Pain

- ✓ **Worship disarms fear.** *Fear thrives on attention. Worship redirects that attention to God's sovereignty.*
- ✓ **Worship redefines perspective.** *When we magnify God, problems lose their false size.*

- ✓ **Worship renews endurance.** *It replenishes strength, not by removing pain, but by revealing purpose.*

Isaiah 61 calls it *"the garment of praise for the spirit of heaviness."* When you wear praise, heaviness loses its grip.

"Worship Under Pressure" – A 5-Day Devotional Reflection

Use this as a personal or group reflection tool for five days.

Day 1 – The Heart of Surrender (Job 1:20–22)

Spend time acknowledging God's sovereignty. Write down one area of your life where you've felt loss or frustration. Then, say aloud:

"The Lord gave, the Lord has taken away; blessed be the name of the Lord."

Let worship begin with trust, not understanding.

Day 2 – The Cave Song (Psalm 34:1–4)

Find a quiet place. Read David's words and write your own "Cave Psalm" — a few sentences of gratitude in the midst of uncertainty.

Day 3 – Midnight Praise (Acts 16:25–26)

Play a worship song at night before bed, especially if your day was hard.

Instead of asking for a way out, thank God for being with you where you are.

Day 4 – Worship as Witness (Philippians 4:4–7)

Reflect on how your attitude in hardship affects those around you. Write one way you can radiate hope at your workplace or home.

Day 5 – Rebuilding Strength (Isaiah 40:31)

Ask God to renew your strength. Journal one testimony from your past — a time when He turned pain into purpose. End with prayer:

"Lord, refine my worship through this pressure. May Your strength be perfected in my weakness."

Closing Thoughts: The Fragrance of Fire

In the end, worship under pressure doesn't just change situations — it changes *us.* When Shadrach, Meshach, and Abednego stepped out of the furnace, the Bible says, *"there was no smell of fire on them"* (Daniel 3:27). That is what worship in pain does — it lets you walk through the fire without smelling like it.

Your trials may bruise you, but they cannot break the worshipper in you. Because worship doesn't depend on your environment — it flows from your encounter.

So, when the pressure mounts, lift your eyes. When the pain deepens, lift your voice. When life feels unfair, lift your hands.

For heaven records no sweeter song than the one sung through tears.

"Though He slay me, yet will I trust Him." — Job 13:15 "I will bless the Lord at all times." — Psalm 34:1

Chapter 13: Reclaiming the Marketplace Altar

"Surely the Lord is in this place, and I did not know it." — Genesis 28:16
"For the earth shall be filled with the knowledge of the glory of the Lord as the waters cover the sea." — Habakkuk 2:14

There was a time when altars were built of stone and wood — visible monuments marking moments of divine encounter. Abraham built them in response to God's promise. Isaac built them to honor covenant. Jacob built one after wrestling with God. Each altar represented a place where heaven met earth, where man met God, and where ordinary ground became holy.

Today, we may no longer carry stones or burn offerings, but the need for altars — sacred spaces where God's presence is intentionally welcomed — remains as real as ever. Only now, these altars must rise not in deserts or mountaintops but in boardrooms, classrooms, hospital corridors, and factory floors.

The call of this generation is clear: to reclaim the marketplace as a place of worship. Not by preaching sermons at our desks, but by turning our workspaces into sanctuaries of prayer, praise, and presence — where God is not an afterthought but the atmosphere.

Jacob's Awakening: The Presence in Unexpected Places

Jacob was running from his past — a deceiver escaping the consequences of his deceit. Exhausted and alone, he lay his head on a stone and drifted into a dream.

In that wilderness, God revealed Himself. A ladder reached from earth to heaven, with angels ascending and descending upon it. When Jacob awoke, he whispered words that still echo across the ages:

"Surely the Lord is in this place, and I did not know it." (Genesis 28:16)

That single realization transformed an ordinary wilderness into a place of worship. Jacob took the stone he had slept on, anointed it with oil, and declared it "Bethel" — *the House of God.*

Jacob didn't build that altar in a temple or synagogue. He built it in a place of exhaustion and uncertainty — the very environment many professionals today inhabit daily. The truth is: God is present in the places we least expect — our offices, clinics, classrooms, studios, and shop floors. We only need to awaken to His presence and mark that place as holy ground.

Nehemiah's Blueprint: Rebuilding with One Hand and Worshipping with the Other

Nehemiah's story is one of sacred restoration within a secular system.

He worked as a cupbearer to a pagan king — a high-ranking government official in a foreign empire. Yet his heart burned for God's purposes. When he heard that Jerusalem's walls lay in ruins, he sought the king's permission to rebuild them.

But Nehemiah's genius lay not just in administration — it lay in the atmosphere he created.

As the workers built, others worshipped. Trumpeters stood beside the builders, and priests prayed as stones were laid. The rebuilding wasn't just a construction project; it was an act of worship.

"Half of my servants worked at construction, while the other half held the spears, shields, bows, and armor… Those who built on the wall, and those who carried burdens, loaded themselves so that with one hand they worked at construction, and with the other held a weapon." (Nehemiah 4:16–17)

That's the picture of reclaiming the marketplace altar — working with one hand and worshipping with the other. Productivity and prayer were not separate; they were partners. The marketplace became their ministry, and their excellence became their offering.

A Modern Parallel: The Story of Rohan and His Office Revival

Rohan worked as a senior analyst in a busy IT firm in Bangalore. Deadlines were relentless, tensions ran high, and the workplace atmosphere was thick with competition and cynicism. Every morning, Rohan would reach his desk early, plug in his headphones, and spend five quiet minutes praying silently for his colleagues, his projects, and his managers.

One day, a junior associate named Priya noticed. *"What do you listen to every morning?"* she asked.

Rohan smiled, *"Not music. I just talk to God about the day."*

Something in that simple answer stirred curiosity. Within weeks, a small group of three colleagues began gathering in a corner conference room for five minutes before work. They read a short Psalm, thanked God for the day, and prayed for wisdom and unity.

Months later, word spread — not as a religious initiative, but as something that genuinely improved morale. Soon, even those from other faiths joined, saying, *"There's peace in that room."*

Over time, subtle yet powerful changes took place. Gossip reduced. Teams collaborated better. Ethical integrity strengthened. Supervisors noticed the shift in workplace culture and commented, "Whatever you're doing, keep doing it — this place feels lighter."

By the end of the year, that office — once marked by burnout and division — had become a marketplace altar, a living testimony that God inhabits even the corporate corridors when invited.

Jesus at the Table: Turning the Ordinary into the Sacred

The New Testament shows Jesus repeatedly transforming ordinary spaces into altars. He didn't confine worship to the temple. He turned a tax collector's house into a place of redemption (Luke 19:1–10), a seashore into a pulpit (Luke 5:3), and a dinner table into a place of communion (Luke 22:19–20).

Everywhere He went, sacredness followed because He carried the presence. Likewise, we are carriers of His presence. The moment a believer steps into an office, a classroom, or a business meeting, the presence of God steps in too. That means your laptop, your meeting room, your construction site — each can become a Bethel if you consciously invite Him in.

Practical Ways to Reclaim the Marketplace Altar

The altar isn't always a physical table — it's an *intentional act of invitation*. Here's how modern believers can transform their workplaces into sacred spaces where heaven touches earth:

1. Begin the Day with Dedication

Before opening your laptop or starting a shift, whisper, *"Lord, this is Your day, Your desk, and Your assignment. Be glorified in my work today."*

Dedication transforms routine into worship. Like Jacob pouring oil on a stone, it marks your workspace as a holy place.

2. Form Workplace Prayer or Reflection Groups

It doesn't need to be elaborate. A 5-minute prayer huddle before work or a short "thankfulness moment" during lunch can shift atmospheres. What matters is consistency.

Remember Jesus' promise: *"Where two or three are gathered in My name, there am I in the midst of them."* (Matthew 18:20)

Even two believers praying quietly in an office corner can open a portal for God's peace to flow.

3. Dedicate Your Work Tools to God

Whether it's a computer, stethoscope, wrench, or microphone — dedicate it as an instrument of excellence and integrity. Pray over your tools:

"Lord, let this tool serve Your purpose and never cause harm or deceit. May Your wisdom flow through my hands."

4. Invite God's Presence before Meetings

Before strategy sessions or client discussions, silently say, *"Holy Spirit, guide our decisions. Let Your wisdom rest in this room."*

You may be surprised how often conflict diffuses or creativity flows when God's presence is invited — even unspoken.

5. Celebrate Testimonies of Transformation

As God begins to move, document stories — improved relationships, ethical turnarounds, breakthroughs. Testimonies fuel faith and inspire others to build their own workplace altars.

When Worship Rebuilds What Was Broken

Nehemiah's builders finished the wall in just 52 days — a task that had seemed impossible for decades. Why? Because worship and work walked hand in hand.

The same principle applies today. When prayer saturates performance, and praise anchors planning, God breathes acceleration into human effort.

Habakkuk prophesied,

"The earth shall be filled with the knowledge of the glory of the Lord as the waters cover the sea." (Habakkuk 2:14)

That glory will not be limited to church pews. It will spill over into stock exchanges, hospitals, schools, and studios — wherever believers dare to rebuild the altar.

Modern Story: Transformation in the Office

At a mid-sized marketing agency in Chennai, the managing director, Meera, faced a moral crisis. A lucrative client demanded deceptive advertising. Torn between conscience and contract, Meera gathered her leadership team and said, *"Before we decide, can we take five minutes to pray for wisdom?"*

It was unusual, but they agreed. Those five minutes became a turning point. They chose integrity over income — and lost the deal. Yet within weeks, new clients came, ones who valued honesty and long-term trust.

Later, a senior team member said, *"I've never prayed in an office before, but I felt peace in that meeting. I think that's what we've been missing."*

That small act of worship — an altar moment in a boardroom — redirected an entire company's trajectory.

Reclaiming Your Ground

Reclaiming the marketplace altar is not about religious performance but spiritual awareness. It's realizing that your desk is your mission field, your conference call is your congregation, and your work ethic is your worship.

When believers begin to live this way — praying quietly before deadlines, showing compassion amid pressure, and walking in integrity despite temptation — the workplace becomes the tabernacle and excellence becomes the incense.

Closing Reflection

The altar doesn't belong to Sunday; it belongs to *everyday.*

Jacob built his in the wilderness. Nehemiah built his among rubble. Jesus built His in the marketplace of humanity.

Now it's your turn.

As you walk into your office, shop floor, or classroom tomorrow, pause and whisper,

"Surely the Lord is in this place."

You might be surprised how heaven answers that whisper with presence, peace, and power — transforming your workplace into Bethel, your daily grind into daily grace, and your labor into a living offering before the Lord.

Conclusion:
Living a Life that Sings

"To Him who sits on the throne and to the Lamb be praise and honor and glory and power, for ever and ever!" — Revelation 5:13
"So whether you eat or drink or whatever you do, do it all for the glory of God."
— 1 Corinthians 10:31

The hum of the city had faded into the night. Offices emptied, shops closed, the noise of traffic now a distant rhythm. Yet somewhere, amidst the quiet, heaven still heard music — not from a church choir or a worship concert, but from lives that had learned to sing even when there was no melody.
That is what this journey has been about — rediscovering the truth that worship is not a song we sing; it's a life we live.
It's not confined to a sanctuary or a Sunday, but expressed in the way we walk through the marketplace on a Monday. It is the sound of hearts aligned with heaven, hands diligent in duty, and spirits sensitive to God's presence in ordinary places.

The Symphony of Everyday Worship
If you've ever stood in an orchestra hall before a concert begins, you'd remember the sound — chaotic tuning, random notes, instruments warming up. Then the conductor raises his hand. Silence falls. A single motion, and suddenly every sound, every string, every drum, every breath finds harmony under one direction.

That's what happens when we surrender every part of life to God — He becomes the Conductor. Our words, our work, our relationships, our giving, our choices — once disconnected — begin to form a divine melody.

Paul captured this beautifully when he said:

"Whether you eat or drink or whatever you do, do all to the glory of God." (1 Corinthians 10:31)

Notice the simplicity of the examples — *eating and drinking.* He wasn't describing temple rituals or public preaching but ordinary acts done with extraordinary awareness of God. That is the essence of worship — a life that sings even in silence.

From the Throne to the Marketplace

In John's vision in Revelation, all creation sings:

"To Him who sits on the throne and to the Lamb be praise and honor and glory and power, forever and ever." (Revelation 5:13)

This song isn't limited to angels or elders in heaven. It includes *"every creature in heaven and on earth."* That means your office desk, your classroom, your kitchen, your farm, your shop — all are arenas where the song of heaven can resound if you choose to glorify God there.

When we align our motives, ethics, and excellence with God's heart, we join that universal chorus. Heaven doesn't just listen to the songs sung on Sunday — it listens to the music of how you work, serve, forgive, and lead.

A Life that Becomes the Song

There's a beautiful quote that says, *"When your life becomes the song, God becomes the audience."*

This means that the truest form of worship isn't when the lights dim and the instruments play, but when your heart quietly says, *"Yes, Lord"* in the middle of pressure, deadlines, and decisions.

Old Testament Harmony: David's Everyday Worship

David's life perfectly captured this. Long before he wrote psalms for the temple choirs, he learned to worship in the fields, caring for sheep, strumming his harp under the stars. Worship didn't begin when he wore the crown — it began when he carried a sling.

Even when he was exiled, running from Saul, David's song didn't stop. He wrote,

"I will bless the Lord at all times; His praise shall continually be in my mouth." (Psalm 34:1)

That *"at all times"* was not poetic exaggeration. It was forged in the wilderness — when he had every reason to complain but chose to worship.

And when David finally became king, he didn't change his rhythm — he simply expanded his platform. The same heart that sang in solitude now led a nation in worship. His life was the song, and God was the audience.

New Testament Rhythm: Paul's Life of Worship

Paul understood this too. He wrote some of his most profound letters not from pulpits but from prison cells. In Philippians 4:4, he said, *"Rejoice in the Lord always. I will say it again: Rejoice!"*

His chains didn't silence his song; they amplified it. The prison became his pulpit. The guards became his congregation. The gospel spread not because of his comfort but because of his consistent worship in every circumstance.

Paul's life teaches us that worship doesn't wait for perfect conditions; it thrives in surrendered hearts. Whether preaching to kings or writing from confinement, he lived what he preached: *"For to me, to live is Christ."* (Philippians 1:21)

Modern Melody: Riya's Quiet Song in the Hospital

Riya, a young nurse in a crowded hospital in Mumbai, began each shift by whispering a prayer over every bed she passed. She never made a show of her faith. Her worship was quiet — changing dressings with compassion, comforting families who grieved, praying silently for patients who were dying.

When the pandemic hit, exhaustion and fear swept through the staff. But Riya's calm spirit became a refuge. Doctors noticed that patients assigned to her ward recovered faster, and staff around her felt strangely uplifted.

One evening, as she left after a long double shift, a colleague asked, *"Riya, how do you stay so peaceful when everything is falling apart?"*

She smiled, eyes tired but radiant, and replied, *"Because every day I get to serve the Healer Himself. This hospital is my temple, and every touch is my worship."*

Riya didn't have a platform, a microphone, or a pulpit. But heaven heard her song. Her life had become the melody — one of love, service, and surrender.

The Eternal Echo of Worship

The beauty of a life of worship is that its echo outlasts the moment. No act of integrity, compassion, or excellence done for God ever goes unheard.

Heaven records every faithful act — the extra mile walked, the word of kindness spoken, the decision to stay pure when compromise seemed easier.
Jesus said,
"Even a cup of cold water given in My name will not lose its reward." (Matthew 10:42)
Every action, however small, becomes a note in the eternal song of worship that rises to the throne of God.

The Marketplace as God's Stage
When you realize your workplace is your worship place, every task — from answering emails to leading teams — becomes part of your offering.
A teacher explaining a difficult concept patiently — that's worship.
A business owner paying fair wages even when competitors cut corners — that's worship.
A driver who refuses a bribe, a manager who encourages his staff, a student who studies with diligence — all are worshippers in disguise.
As Paul wrote to the Colossians: *"Whatever you do, whether in word or deed, do it all in the name of the Lord Jesus."* (Colossians 3:17)
The goal is no longer applause from men, but approval from heaven. Worship becomes a way of life, not a once-a-week ritual.

Final Reflection: Your Life, God's Song
Heaven's greatest desire is not just to hear your voice — but to hear your *life*. Your decisions, your kindness, your perseverance, your humility — they form a song that rises before God day and night.
When the world sees you working with joy, forgiving with grace, and standing firm in truth, they hear a

melody that cannot be ignored — the sound of worship in human form.

Like a symphony, your life will have moments of silence, tension, and triumph. But in the hands of the Master Conductor, every note — even the broken ones — will find its place in the divine composition.

A Closing Commissioning Prayer

Lord, make my marketplace Your temple. Let my desk become an altar, my work a song of worship, my decisions a testimony of Your wisdom, my relationships a fragrance of Your love. Teach me to walk in reverence, to work with excellence, to serve with humility, and to live with gratitude.

May every action, every conversation, and every heartbeat bring glory to You.

And when the world looks at my life, may they hear heaven's music through me.

In Jesus' name, Amen.

When the final page is turned and the lights dim on every stage, may heaven still hear your song — not from your lips alone, but from your life.

Because in the end, a true worshipper doesn't just sing songs of praise — they *become* one. Your life becomes the song. And God… becomes the audience.

About the Author
'GERARD ASSEY'

Gerard Assey is a Graduate in Economics, a PGD in Management (HRD) and holds a Doctorate in Leadership. Gerard holds several International Qualifications in Sales, Debt Collection, Training & Teaching, and is a 'Fellow' of the prestigious 'Institute of Sales & Marketing Management'-UK, a Certified NLP Practitioner, a 'Certified Trainer', an 'Accredited Management Teacher-Behavioral Sciences', a 'Certified Competency Facilitator', a 'Certified Management Consultant'- (the International credentials of a professional management consultant, awarded in accordance with global standards of the ICMCI); and a Certification from the University of Michigan in 'Successful Negotiation: Essential Strategies and Skills'

He is also a Member of the 'National Association of Sales Professionals' backed with several years experience in varied industries, both in India and Overseas. He also holds an 'Etiquette Consultant' Certification from the USA (by Sue Fox, Author of Best Seller: 'Business Etiquette for Dummies'. She has trained some of the top celebrities' world over). He was also a recipient of a scholarship for extensive training in Japan on 'Corporate Management for India'.

Gerard Assey is 'Founder & Chief Corporate Trainer' of the Group: **'Citius, Altius, Fortius Unlimited'**- an organization that **celebrated 20 years of Glorious Service** in 2021, focusing on 3 Core Competencies:

People. Performance. Profit; in functional areas of Sales & Marketing, HR & Organizational Development, covering Recruitment, Training & Consultancy!

Having managed organizations with large Sales Forces in India & Overseas, his specialization cover extensive areas of Sales Training (All levels - Presentation, Negotiation, Key/ Strategic Accounts Management & Managerial Skills for all sectors), Bid Proposal/ Capture Planning/ Management Trainings, Retail Sales, Customer Service & Customer Retention Programs, Training for Prevention & Collection of Debt, Self & Personal Development Programs (Time Management, Teamwork & Team Building, Business Etiquette & Personal Grooming, Leadership & Managerial Skills, People Management Skills, Train-the-Trainer etc), including preparation of Custom-designed Business Manuals for Internal (HR, Induction, and Sales etc) & External use (Instruction, User Manuals).

Gerard has successfully conducted over 6495 Trainings & Workshops (as of Jan '26) all across India, Middle East, Africa, Europe & S.E. Asia. Besides public programs conducted regularly, both in India & Overseas, he has some of the top names as clients whom he services from Single Owners to large Public & Government undertakings, covering all sectors, for their in-house needs.

His website: www.CollectionSkills.com is the only one in this part of the world to be featured in the 'Collections & Credit Risk Magazine-USA' under 'Who's Who in Training' and ranks TOP, along with other websites listed below on most search engines.

Gerard is author of 217 Books already (Jan 2026), all the books being available on all online platforms and outlets as E-books and Paperbacks

A few of our business related books:

1. Bite-sized Bits on Commonsense Management
2. Heart to Heart on Life's Principles'
3. How to become a Successful Manager
4. The Sales Professionals' Master Workbook of S.Y.S.T.E.M.S
5. The Professional Business Email Etiquette Handbook & Guide
6. The Professional Business Video-Conferencing Etiquette Handbook & Guide
7. Professional Presentation Skills
8. Exceptional Customer Service
9. Professional Tele-Marketing Skills
10. Professional Debt Collection Skills
11. The G.R.E.A.T. Sales & Service Workbook
12. Sales Training Advantage for Results (*The Ultimate Sales Training Manual to enable you stand out as a S.T.A.R.*)
13. CEO Daily Planner & Organizer
14. The Sales Professionals' Master Daily Planner
15. The Professional Debt Collector's Master Daily Planner
16. My Daily Planner & Organizer
17. MY EMERGENCY INFORMATION RECORD (Family Emergency & Peace of Mind Planner)
18. The Ultimate Therapist & Counselors Planner and Organizer
19. Building an Ethical Workplace
20. Managing Relationships at Work
21. Managing Business Meetings Effectively
22. Effective Delegation Skills
23. Goal Setting for Success
24. B2B Selling by Email
25. Professional Business Etiquette & Grooming
26. Dining Etiquette & Table Manners
27. Effective Networking Skills
28. Grooming, Etiquette & Manners for Teens, Young Adults & Future Leaders
29. Inter-Personal Skills
30. Get Ready, Get Hired!
31. Selling in a Recession
32. Effective Receivables Management in an Economic Downturn!
33. Real Estate & Property Sales Training
34. Credit Sales & Accounts Receivable Management

35. Selling Skills for Real Estate & Property Advisors
36. Take G.R.E.A.T. C.A.R.E!
37. Spa, Salon & Health Club Selling Skills
38. Selling Travel, Holiday & MICE Services
39. Selling Skills for Spa's, Salons & Health Clubs
40. Retailing in Salons & Spas
41. Selling Holiday, Vacation, Tours & Packages
42. The Power of Sales Referrals
43. Selling Luxury
44. Technical Selling Skills
45. Financial Advisors Sales Training
46. Dealing with Burnout at Work Monopolize Your Markets
47. Selling to Affluent Customers
48. Growing up with Grace
49. Financial Selling Skills
50. *The Effective Manager's Guide: Key Skills to Thrive*
51. From Aspiring to Inspiring: A Guide for New Managers on the Rise
52. The Power of Focus
53. Selling with Integrity: Sell Like Jesus The Perfect Role Model!
54. 31 Habits of Champions: Your 31-Day Journey to Greatness
55. Rejecting Grasshopper Talk: From Grasshopper to Giant-Killer-*Defeating Giants Daily!*
56. Navigate the AI-Powered Future of Bid & Proposals: Up-Skill to Stay Relevant with Alternative Career Paths & Opportunities
57. Hiring Sales Winners
58. Present with Impact
59. Success Unlocked: *Breaking Free from Habits that Hold You Back*
60. Complaints to Cheers, Feedback to Gold: Mastering Complaints Management
61. Thriving Together: *Cultivating Diversity, Equity, and Inclusion*
62. Coaching Skills for Sales Managers
63. Soaring to Success in Business & Leadership: Swifter, Higher, Stronger!
64. From Classroom to Podium: A Student's Guide to Powerful Public Speaking & Presentation Skills
65. Developing Self-Discipline
66. The CEO's 31-Day Power Plan: Unlocking Success through Essential Traits

67. Credibility Matters
68. A Winning Attitude
69. Bid & Proposal Management Using AI
70. Sales Forecasting: A Practical & Proven Guide to Strategic Sales Forecasting
71. Elevate & Energize: *50 Dynamic & Fun Activities for Peak Workplace Morale*
72. 'Sales SOS! Sales on Fire! *30 Days to Conquer Chaos & the Nightmares of Success!'*
73. Mastering Sales Managerial Skills: *Building High-Performing Teams & Driving Exceptional Results*
74. Eagle-Eyed Leadership: Unleashing the Power of 31 Lessons from Eagles
75. The Ultimate Employee Training Guide: *Training Today, Leading Tomorrow*
76. Being More Accountable at Work
77. Creating a Culture of Continuous Improvement
78. Effective Questioning & Listening Skills
79. The Power of Value Selling
80. The Growth Mindset
81. Mastering Professional Help Desk Skills
82. The Power to Lead with Empathy
83. Being Prepared: The Key to Unlocking Success
84. Youthful Spark-Youth Energizers, Activities and Games-Igniting the Fun in Youth
85. Ignite your Motivation for Success
86. Elevate Your Executive Presence: *Your Roadmap to Executive Excellence*
87. Smart Decisions: *Mastering Problem Solving with Strategic Solutions for Business Success*
88. Strategic Planning: *Developing and Implementing Strategic Plans to Achieve Long-Term Business Goals*
89. The Power of Stay Interviews
90. Developing G.R.I.T.
91. Adaptability
92. Diagnosis- *A Key Skill for Leadership*
93. The Burnout-Proof Salesperson: *The Master Guide to Preventing Stress & Burnout*- Strategies for Thriving in Sales
94. Learning from Failure: *Keys to Success*
95. Customer Success Management
96. Overcoming the Killers of Motivation
97. The C-Suite Code: *Mastering Skills for Executive Excellence'*

98. Dealing with Difficult Customers
99. Unlocking Your Potential: Mastering the Top 20 Life Skills for a Brighter Future
100. Nurturing Tomorrow's Leaders: *Essential Soft Skills Every Child Must Learn*
101. Lively & Fun Party Games for Seniors & Elders
102. Role Playing for Sales Champions: From Practice to Performance
103. Fun and Exciting Party Games for Kids
104. Case Studies for Sales
105. Role-Playing for Unbeatable Customer Service
106. Case Studies in Customer Service
107. Case Studies in Winning Negotiations
108. Case Studies in Management & Leadership
109. Case Studies in Human Resources & Talent Management
110. CEO Success Blueprint: The Essential Toolkit for CEOs and C-Level Executives
111. The Salesperson's Self-Coaching Guide: *Master Your Own Self-Coaching Plan for Success*
112. Overcoming Procrastination: *Your Ultimate Guide to Stop Delaying and Start Living Your Best Life*
113. When True Colors Are Exposed: *The Journey to Unmasking Humanity*
114. Life-Changing Habits for Teens: Teen Success Blueprint for a Bright Future
115. Workplace Stress-Free: *Proven Strategies to Thrive at Work and Beyond*
116. Objection Overruled: *The Ultimate Guide to Turning 'No' into 'Yes'*
117. Building Strong Teams: *A Comprehensive Guide to Team Building*
118. Ethical & Moral Leadership in Business: *Eliminating Unethical Practices & Building a Culture of Trust & Integrity*
119. Rising Strong: Building Positive: High Self-Esteem for a Fulfilling Life-*A Practical Guide for Students, Employees, Leaders & Entrepreneurs*
120 The Cheerful Mindset: Cultivating a Joyful Outlook Everyday
121. Leading Through Crisis: Case Studies on Crisis Management
122. Selling Beyond the Algorithms

From the Ministry side, Gerard graduated in the very first batch of Charis Bible College-India & had for over 9 years served as a Part-time Faculty at Charis Bible College-Chennai (Andrew Wommack Ministries-Colorado, USA).
He also holds a Diploma in Worship (a subject closest to his heart) from the JSOW and is also a graduate of the Advanced Mentorship Program (AMP) and the Circle Of Ministerial Engagement (C.O.M.E.) of Prophet Jerome Fernando and a Spiritual Son of the Esteemed Prophet.
An accomplished author of several Secular & Christian Books, Gerard has been on the board of a few international organizations and boasts of being the SON of the MOST HIGH GOD: An ordinary guy following an extraordinary GOD!

...And some of his most recent Christian Books being:

1. A Bouquet of Praises for My KING
2. Christian Jokes for the Serious Religious' Folks!
3. Jesus Healed You!
4. Praise24Ever! (also in Tamil version)
5. The 5G Network of GOD
6. Building Faith over F.E.A.R- FACE EVERYTHING AND RISE with JESUS
7. Hebrew and Greek Praise and Worship Words
8. Godly Mothers' and Grandmothers' Bible Story time for Kids!
9. Miracles of Jesus in Pictures
10. Raise your Praise all 365 Days
11. Thanking GOD with an Attitude of Gratitude
12. Meditating on the Attributes of GOD
13. Puppet Scripts
14. Alcohol Ruins, JESUS Reforms, Renews & Restores!
15. Habakkuk 2:2 Christian Daily Journal, Planner & Organizer
16. ABC of GOD's Word for Handwriting Practice
17. Daily Bible Verse Handwriting Practice (Building Godly Character & Faith through Cursive Handwriting Practice!)
18. Guiding Light: Fun & Faith-Building Bible Activities for Children
19. Rejecting Grasshopper Talk: From Grasshopper to Giant-Killer-*Defeating Giants Daily!*
20. Teen Titans of Faith: *Building Courage, Determination & Christ-like-Esteem*
21. I AM Empowered: *Unleashing Divine Power with Positive Declarations*

22. Be A Solution Provider-*From Passion to Purpose*: *A Biblical Guide to Being the Answer to the World!*
23. Miracles of JESUS
24. Parables of Jesus for a Meaningful Life!
25. A Grateful Heart: Importance of Sharing Testimonies of GOD's Grace
26. Melodies of Worship to JESUS: 31 Songs of Praise & Worship From My Heart to HIS!
27. I AM SO BLESSED!
28. My Daily Cup of Energizer
29. 31 Leadership Lessons *from* Jesus- *The Supreme Leader*
30. Peace Amidst Storms: A Biblical Guide to Conquering S.T.R.E.S.S.
31. Rise Above: 20 Biblical Eagle Lessons for Life's Triumphs
32. Godly Goal Setting: *The FAITHFUL Blueprint for a Purpose-Driven Life*
33. The Profound Attributes of our Mighty GOD: Understanding the 10S's of the Almighty
34. Worship Now, Worship Forever: *A Journey from Earthly Praise to Eternal Glory*
35. Unceasing Praise & Worship: *365 Days to Worship the King*
36. The ROAR Within: *Living with Purpose and Authority through the Power of the Holy Spirit*
37. From Potential to Purpose: Unlocking and Multiplying Your Talents & Gifts for Kingdom Impact
38. Songs from the Heart: *Worshipping GOD in Your Own Tune & Melody*
39. Awakening Praise & Worship: Hebrew & Greek Words to Raise Your Praise
40. Sing a NEW Song to the LORD Everyday: *Daily Devotions of Praise & Worship to Lift Your Heart & Glorify HIS Name*
41. *The* A.R.O.M.A. of True Worship: *Creating Worship That Delights God*
42. Becoming A Kingdom Champion: *Embracing God's Call for a Life of Purpose & Victory*
43. The Busy Businessman's Daily Devotional: 366 Crisp Truths to Start Your Day Strong
44. The Teacher's Heart: *Daily Devotions for Educators*
45. Anchored! *A 31-Day Devotional for Students Facing Life's Challenges*
46. Suddenly! Unlocking Unorthodox Breakthroughs through Unusual Worship
47. Overcoming Adversity: *Lessons from the Bible for Modern*

Challenges

48. LORD, Don't do it without me
49. Kingdom Leadership: *Biblical Principles for Modern Leaders*
50. Heartprints of God- *Growing God's Way:* Daily Devotions for Kids to Shine Bright
51. Send Judah First: Let your Praises Go up First to See the Mighty Move of GOD
52. DIVINE MOMENTS: *Recognizing, Embracing, Preparing, and Walking into Life-Changing Encounters with God*
53. Be a Builder in the Kingdom: *The C.E.M.E.N.T. Guide to Creating a Lasting Legacy*
54. Unshakable: *Pillars of Godly Womanhood* (Pillars of Faith That Changed History)
55. Lead Like a Shepherd: *14 Essential Traits for Pastoral Excellence*
56. The Worship Leader's Arsenal: *Powerful Exhortations to Ignite Thanksgiving, Praise & Worship*
57. Women of UnShakable Faith: *31-Day Devotional for Strength, Purpose & Influence*
58. Called to Teach: *A Complete 10-Week Training Guide for Impactful VBS Teachers*
59. Strumming for the KING: Cowboy Songs of Faith & Fire
60. The Ultimate Youth Camp Playbook: *50 Bible-Centered Indoor Games to Engage, Equip, and Empower Teens*
61. Glad in HIS Presence: *David's Revelation of GOD's Love & Mercy*
62. The Spirit Behind the Sound: *52 Devotionals for Worship Teams*
63. THE COWBOY'S COMPASS: *Riding the Trail of Faith with Grit & Grace*
64. Worship as My Weapon: *Living Victoriously through the Power of Praise*
65. A Worshipper Always Wins*: Living a Life of Victorious Worship*
66. Worship That Leads to the Throne: *Practical Strategies for Worship Leaders to Inspire Their Team & Usher People into God's Presence*
67. Worship as Warfare: *Conquering through the Sound of Surrender*
68. Watchmen on the Walls: *A 31-Day Devotional for Worship Teams*
69. KINGDOM BUSINESS: *52 Biblical Principles for GODLY*

Leadership & Wise Decisions

70. From Evening to Morning: *Rediscovering GOD's Sacred Hours*
71. Waves of Glory: *Worship through Dance, Flags, Staff & Sound*
72. WORSHIP TEAM BUILDER: *Guiding Your Team from Formation to Fruitfulness*
73. The Worship Leader's Master Training Manual
74. Skits for the King: Children's Plays for Every Church Occasion
75. Unbreakable: Building Strong Marriages and Families God's Way *(From Vows to Victory)*
76. Songs for my King: *A 31-Day Journey of Praise*
77. Building Powerful Children: *Raising a Generation That Will Shape the Future for God*
78. Character Before Chords: *The Heart of the True Worshipper*
79. 365 Days Before His Throne: A Worshipper's Daily Declarations
80. Broken to Built: *How GOD Restores Lives, Heals Hearts & Uses Broken People for HIS Glory*
81. Fear Did Not Come from God: *Discerning the Source, Dismantling the Stronghold & Walking in Power, Love & a Sound Mind*
82. THE GOD OF BEGINNINGS: *Positioning Your Life for What God Is About to Start*
83. HEALED ALREADY: IT IS FINISHED! Receiving What the Cross Has Completed!
84. A.D.D.E.D. Y.E.A.R.S. When God Overrules the Clock, the Diagnosis, and the Final Word
85. HALLELUJAH -The Sound That Heaven Understands *(Building a Life of Pure Praise)*
86. Worship in the Marketplace, Worship Beyond the Walls: *(Turning Work into Worship)*

Besides regularly contributing to business & trade journals, including international ones such as the 'Creative Training Techniques' and the 'Sales News' of the U.S.A, He is also a member of several prestigious bodies & trade associations, having participated in many Conferences & Workshops in India & Overseas.

Prior to his last assignment of leading & managing a large MNC as head, Gerard had a 3-year stint in the Middle East as a Consultant with a leading British Consultancy Firm.

As the past 'Official Country Representative' for the International Business Award- 'THE STEVIES'-(the business world's own Oscar) for about 4 years- he ensured a few Indian companies that qualify for the same every year!

Gerard can be contacted at:
Email: training@Sales-Training.in,training@CollectionSkills.com
Websites:
www.Sales-Training.in
www.EtiquetteWorks.in
www.CollectionSkills.com
www.RetailSalesTraining.in
www.SalesTrainingIndia.com
www.ManualPreparation.com
www.TrainingWithPuppets.com
www.FirstContactAcademy.com
www.SalesAndMarketingRecruiter.com

www.ingramcontent.com/pod-product-compliance
Ingram Content Group UK Ltd.
Pitfield, Milton Keynes, MK11 3LW, UK
UKHW021340190726
13845UKWH00027B/648

9 788199 301733